SIX DOTS FOR ASIA

Other titles by the same author:

God's Adventurer – A Biography of Hudson Taylor
No Way Back – The Story of Rupert Clarke
Pilgrim in China – An Autobiographical Account of Life in China
Sadhu Sundar Singh – A Biography

SIX DOTS
FOR ASIA

'Then will the eyes of the blind be opened . . .'
(*Isaiah 35:5*, NIV)

Phyllis Thompson

OM publishing
CARLISLE, UK

© Phyllis Thompson 1995

First published 1995

01 00 99 98 97 96 95   7 6 5 4 3 2 1

OM Publishing is an imprint of Send the Light Ltd.,
P.O. Box 300, Carlisle, Cumbria CA3 0QS, U.K.

British Library Cataloguing in Publication Data
Thompson, Phyllis
Six Dots For Asia
I. Title
266.00954

ISBN 1-85078-176-1

Typeset by Photoprint, Torquay, Devon
and Printed in the U.K. by Cox and Wyman Ltd., Reading

Contents

Acknowledgements

My sincere thanks are due to Westcountry Television for supplying the full script of their interview with Rona Gibb.

To Miss Jeanette Short for information and literature about work among the blind in India.

To Rev. P. T. Chandapilla for information and his impressions of Tony & Rona Gibb's early years in India.

To Professor Don Rogers for information about his computer programming.

To Mrs Iris Bellchamber who so patiently typed up the manuscript for me.

Thanks to Tony and Rona Gibb for all their help, and for supplying copies of all their letters to prayer partners.

To Mary Vogt, at whose suggestion this book was written.

Foreword

I commend this book with great pleasure, not only because I have known Rona and Tony Gibb for many years, but also because the work that they are engaged in has a story worth the telling. Rona, registered blind, and with the lovely gift of making friends; Tony, a gifted organiser, handyman, and with wide business experience; Professor Don Rogers with a brilliant mind and grasp of languages, and awareness of what the computer may achieve in putting scripts of any language into Braille; three people whose meeting has, under God, brought Compass Braille into being.

Phyllis Thompson has skilfully woven many strands together, showing how a loving God, from very small and unlikely beginnings, has since brought together a team of dedicated people, placed them in a small town in Devonshire, and is using them to begin to get the scriptures in Braille to the people in Asia.

(India alone, has 900 million people, many different languages, and 10 million who are blind.)

It is a colossal task, being made possible through the modern technology of computers, and the latest in Braille printers. Steve Brown (in charge of Braille production), and the staff in Moretonhampstead, have the help and support of local Christians in helping to make the finished product—Bible books —and mailing them overseas. Rona and Tony's vision is that one day in the countries of Asia, there will be many presses like Compass Braille that will be able to meet local needs.

The Bible tells the story of five loaves and two fishes that fed five thousand. This book tells the story of how *Six Dots for Asia*, feeds millions!

Tim Buckley
April, 1995

Prologue

'But who will produce the books for us?' exclaimed the Professor, thumping the arm of his chair vehemently, 'My computer program to produce Hindi braille is ready to run.' He paused for a moment and looked across at Tony and Rona Gibb, then went on, 'And it can be used not only for Hindi. It can produce all the Indian languages!'

It was a great claim, but his listeners knew it was justified. They had approached him about the matter years before, when they heard that he had compiled a computer program to produce Russian braille from the print script. Their immediate reaction had been, 'If it can be done for Russian, why not for Indian languages?', and his response to their request had been enthusiastic when he knew they had Bibles in braille in mind. He had put in many hours of hard work on the program, but the problem had been the difficulty of using Romanized script for Indian languages. The breakthrough! had come when, on a visit to the Wycliffe Bible Translators, he learned of a new computer program which might be versatile enough to use for braille. A copy of it was given to him free of charge, and within two or three weeks he had the basis of a program to convert Hindi script directly into braille. During 1988 he had worked steadily on this, and had explored the possibility of working on other Indian languages – and now, on this bleak December morning he was sitting with his wife in their Sussex home, announcing to the Gibbs that he had accomplished what he had set out to do, and posing his question, 'Who will produce the Scriptures in braille for India?'

He knew before he spoke that there was no easy answer. Braille presses around the world were running at full capacity, for modern computer technology had revolutionized production, and there was more work waiting to be done than could be dealt with. The production of complete Bibles in Hindi, Urdu, Tamil, Gujerati – some fourteen languages at least, was a colossal task, and as far as the Gibbs, or he himself knew, there was no organization that would take it on.

But the need remained. Tony and Rona had just returned from a visit to India, with moving stories of the longing of blind Christians for the Bible that they could read for themselves, in the only way possible – through the tips of their fingers. It had been challenging to listen to Indian friends announcing,

'There are 500 blind people in Maharashtra that I could pass the books on to individually. . .'

'I have 1,500 blind people waiting to read the Bible in Gujerati. I can distribute 1,500 copies of any gospel you can send me within a month of receiving them, and I could tell you exactly where each copy had gone to. . .'

'We get letters every week asking for braille Bibles in the Indian languages. . .'

'Our blind Tamil friends want to know what is in the Old Testament. They have never read any of it. They only have part of the New Testament. . .'

And time and time again the question had come, 'Can't you do something about it?'

What could they do? On the one hand was the computer program that now made possible in days production that had previously taken years. On the other hand, distributors were poised ready to dole out Scriptures in braille as soon as they arrived. But between the two was a hiatus. Production was the bottleneck.

As the four of them sat together discussing the problem the question seemed unanswerable, until the conversation took an unexpected turn. The Professor, in his eagerness to provide those blind believers in India with what they longed for, suggested that he himself might become involved in the actual process of the braille production set up a unit right there in Bexhill. . .

It was at that point his wife broke in.

'No,' she said firmly. 'Don already works far too hard. He's often working on his computers until the early hours. He simply has not the time to set up a braille press. I think that should be Tony's work.'

The words were followed by what Rona later described as a stunned silence. She could not see her husband's face, but with that acute sixth sense of hers she knew just what he was feeling. The words had come to him like a bolt from the blue. It had never occurred to him to become responsible for a braille unit, although he knew all about installing it and running it. Perhaps his very knowledge of what was involved contributed to the dismay he felt at the challenge of Lilian's pronouncement. To be responsible for obtaining and installing the braille machinery, for ordering the equipment, for storing the paper and the completed Bibles, for employing staff – why it would take hundreds of thousands of pounds! He explained all this when he had recovered his breath, adding that they'd need a building to house it – one completed Bible in braille occupied a shelf four feet long. . .

'We'd soon be squeezed out of house and home if we started it in Sunnymead!

The conversation petered to a pause, but the sense of responsibility they all felt remained, and quietly, in the silence, someone said,

'Let's pray about it.'

And that was when Rona had her vision.

More than any of the others she could feel for those blind believers in India. She understood so completely their longing to run their fingers again and again over the words that spoke as no other words did, to their hearts. Had not the Lord some plan to provide them with that for which they yearned? A place where Bibles could be produced for them?

There was. While the others were praying she saw it quite clearly. It was an empty building in one of the narrow winding streets in the very town in Devon where she and Tony were living. She had passed it innumerable times when she had made her way carefully along the pavement from Sunnymead up to the town centre to do her shopping. She had only seen it as a creamy blur as she went by, but in her vision it was quite clear, with its high windows and arched doorway. As the others were praying the vision filled her mind, and when they had finished she said rather hesitantly,

'You know, there's an old empty Methodist chapel in Cross Street in Moretonhampstead. Could that be used to produce braille Bibles for India?'

1

Rona's School Days

Not until Rona was eighteen years old did she fully realize how hard a thing it is to be blind. As she found her way along the corridors of the Teachers' Training College to which she had been admitted, the only myopic one in the whole student body, she wondered if she could make it. She knew that she was there as a sort of experiment, there had never been a blind student before, and that if she failed there would never be another. The thought that the opening or closing of the door of opportunity for others depended on her only added to her burden, and there were times when she buried her head in her hands in the solitude of her bedroom, and wept.

She had never been so alone before. Although she was an only child her parents had seen to it that she was neither coddled nor isolated. Her father himself was blind, but supported his family by piano tuning, travelling confidently around to the homes of his clients, living a normal life with good relationships among friends and neighbours. Probably he was not so dismayed as was his wife when they realized that their baby could not see.

For Rona's mother it had been a severe shock – somehow it was something she had never anticipated. 'If I'd known, I wouldn't have had a baby', she often said. But she loved her child, and brought her up in just the same way as if she could see. From an early age the little girl was expected to fold her clothes before getting into bed, help to lay the table and wash up afterwards. She was sent out to play with other children, and when she was old enough she went along the road to do a little shopping, so she was quite accustomed to going out alone.

Education had presented the biggest problem. Eye operations at a very early age had resulted in enough sight to distinguish between dark and light and identify blurred outlines of objects when they came within her limited range of vision. If a page with writing or pictures was held within an inch of her eyes she could even discern what was on it, though it was a strain to do so, and she couldn't concentrate for long. The headmistress of the small private infants school which she attended wisely explained to Mr. and Mrs. Waller that their little girl was so visually handicapped that she ought to be taught braille – which naturally was not on the curriculum. So at the age of six the Education Authorities agreed to move Rona, but only to a partially sighted school in Berkshire where she could not see the blackboard, or even the books from which the children learned to read, resulting in her forgetting all she had learnt. Her parents were told she was educationally sub-normal.

Then she was transferred to Wavertree School for the Blind in Liverpool, where she was very happy, made plenty of friends, went home every other weekend – and mastered the ingenious system by which blind people the world over can read through their finger tips. She learned to read and write braille.*

The seed thought of braille was conceived in the unlikely setting of the battlefield. A French army officer devised a scheme of tangible writing by using dots instead of letters for night time communications. This was in 1819, the very year when a little boy named Louis Braille entered the National Institute for Blind Children in Paris. The lad heard about this 'night writing' as it was called, remembered the

---

* The braille system of writing for and by blind people which is universally accepted, consists of six raised dots on embossed paper, arranged in two vertical rows of three, placed side by side, as in a domino. These can be used in a code of 63 characters made up of one to six of the dots arranged in different positions in the 'cell'.

Examples:

Originally it was an alphabetical code for France but then spread throughout the world and in many languages it is used phonetically.

feel of the brass studs in his father's harnessing business, worked on the idea, and at the age of fifteen produced the six dot 'cell' system which was first published five years later, and with a few variations and modifications has been used ever since.

Rona learned a lot more than braille at Wavertree School. She learned to amuse herself playing make-believe games with the very few toys she possessed. (It was not long after the end of the Second World War, and toys were scarce in those days.) Even more important, she learned to make friends. The two terms in the school in Berkshire had turned her in upon herself, for most of the pupils there had better sight than she, and with the strange cruelty children can display, had often teased, even bullied her.

There was an altogether different atmosphere at Wavertree, and Rona was conscious of it right from the start. Within a week she had linked up with Dorothy, who arrived on the same day, and forty-five years later the two were still in touch. Rona early developed a propensity for keeping friends as well as making them. When the time came to move to another school they both passed the entrance exam to Chorleywood College, and went there together.

It was at Chorleywood that she learned, along with the other blind pupils, how to use a white cane, how to find her way about by memorizing distances and landmarks like hedges and gates, lamp-posts and pillar boxes, distinguishing sounds, how to go shopping. Smells were a help with shopping – she knew when she came to a butcher's shop, or a baker's, or a green-grocers. Each had its distinctive odour. She joined the poultry club so that she could learn how to keep chickens, had her own little garden plot, even climbed trees, and rode on the rather aged ponies provided by the school.

But perhaps the most important event in Rona's time at Chorleywood College, although she certainly did not realize it, was the arrival of a new teacher – Jeanette Short. Jeanette was only twenty-two when she took up her position as a form mistress and maths teacher. It was her first experience of teaching blind children, and she felt a little apprehensive. She talked about it to the headmistress, who reassured her, and then singled out one of the pupils for special mention.

'Rona Waller will help you', she said. 'Rona is not outstanding academically – just average – but she's friendly and outgoing. Not shy or giggly. She knows where things are kept, and what ought to be done, that sort of thing. Her mother has trained her well. She'll help you.'

Jeanette settled in at Chorleywood College without much difficulty, and soon became one of the most popular form teachers – except in maths classes! – because she showed a genuine interest in her pupils quite apart from their academic studies. She invited them into her room, encouraged them when they were worried or homesick, and spent a lot of her free time reading aloud to them. These reading sessions were particularly welcomed. Jeanette could introduce them to books that had never, and probably never would be, produced in braille.

Rona listened avidly. Many of the books and articles were about life and people in other countries, particularly India, and when she learned that Jeanette herself was hoping to go to that very country and work among blind people, her interest deepened.

Meanwhile, she herself was in her last term in Chorleywood College, and after the summer vacation would be launching out into an entirely new environment as the only myopic student in a Teacher Training College, and she felt the need for some preparation for this experience. All her life, apart from the two unhappy terms as a little girl in the Berkshire boarding school, she had lived with her parents, or with others as visually handicapped as herself. What would it be like to live among what could be termed 'ordinary people'? She longed to be 'ordinary' herself, and as she talked about it to some of the other girls in her class, she found they were feeling the same. Looking forward to the summer vacation they agreed they wanted to try having a holiday without their parents. But where could they go, and how could it be arranged? Then someone said,

'Let's ask Miss Short. Perhaps she'll be able to help us.' So to Miss Short they went and she soon made a suggestion.

'There are several organizations I know of that run camps – sort of houseparties – for young people', she said. 'Perhaps I could arrange for you to go to one of those.' Then she added more slowly,

'I'd better explain that they are Christian organizations – there would be prayers, and a meeting with a

Bible talk each evening probably. You ought to be prepared for that . . .'

'Yes, that would be all right', they responded readily enough. As far as Rona was concerned, she felt she would fit into a Christian organization quite naturally. It had been compulsory to go to church when in Chorleywood College, confirmation classes were offered there every year, her mother had encouraged her to be confirmed, and so, as a member of the Anglican church she had no doubt as to her own suitability to go to a Christian camp.

The difficulty for Jeanette was to find one that was willing to accept visually handicapped girls. One after another of the organizations to which she applied wrote back to say that they regretted they had not the facilities to accommodate them. It was disappointing and humiliating for the girls to realize that there seemed no place for them in ordinary society. Educationally and intellectually they were up to the standard of their sighted contemporaries, they knew how to conduct themselves in social events, their financial resources presented no problem — there was no suggestion of their expecting reductions in fees.

But they could not see. They would be a liability in a house party. The door was closed to them.

Then one day Jeanette, rather excitedly, told them she had good news.

'I can take you all to the Ambassador House Party to be held at Overstone School in Northamptonshire', she said triumphantly. 'It's run by a missionary society called the Bible and Medical Missionary

Fellowship that works in India. They say they will
welcome you – and as you are a bit older than most
of the schoolgirls who will be there, they'll put you
in the same dormitories as the junior officers.' Then
she told them what they should take with them –
swim suits and towels, summer frocks with a
raincoat and a warm jacket in case of bad weather,
good walking shoes, and so on. One thing only
presented a problem. As it was a Christian house
party everyone would be expected to bring a Bible –
but a Bible in braille would be about fifty times
bigger and heavier than an ordinary Bible, and it
would be too much for them to carry in addition to
their suitcases. Even if they took one between the
four of them it would be too heavy and cumbersome.
It was agreed that they would have to do without
Bibles of their own and just be prepared to listen
very attentively when passages from Scripture were
read out aloud. So off they went for the holiday that
Rona was to remember for the rest of her life. Many
years later she described in a television interview
what happened.

'It was a huge school, and we did all the usual
things that one does on holiday, but as it was
Christian we used to have a special time of fellowship every evening. I noticed that the other young
people of my age, classed as junior officers, seemed
to have a sort of special relationship with God that I
didn't have.

'I believed in God and believed in Jesus and that he
died on a cross, but it was rather like I believed that

Queen Elizabeth the First was the Queen of England. I didn't have the kind of personal relationship that they had, and I remember feeling a bit as though they were on one side of a wall and I was on the other.

'However, I didn't think too much about it until one evening when the person leading the meeting (her name was Barbara Spanner) explained very simply what it meant to be a real Christian. She said that first of all you need to admit you are a sinner.

'Secondly, you needed to believe that Jesus Christ died for you.

'Thirdly, you needed to commit your life to Christ.

'Well, it was a bit of a shock to me. Actually, I wanted to do the third thing. I really wanted to commit my life, because I sort of realized that unless I had Christ in my life I wasn't going to make very much of it. But I certainly didn't like the thought of admitting that I was a sinner.

'I didn't think I was a sinner. I thought I was a nice, helpful sort of person. I always tried to look after people, be nice, do nice things. But she went on to explain that admitting you were a sinner meant knowing you weren't perfect, and that perfection was the standard God expected of us all.

'That helped a bit! As for believing in Jesus, well I did believe in him, that he had died on a cross, but it had never dawned on me before, I had never realized it was actually for me, that I was personally involved – that my sin had put him there.'

Even that vague realization might not have persuaded Rona to go any farther had the one leading the meeting not announced they were now going to sing a chorus.

> There's a way back to God from the dark paths
>   of sin,
> There's a door that is open and you may go in,
> At Calvary's cross is where you begin
> When you come as a sinner to Jesus.

'We'll sing that together', the speaker said, then added emphatically, 'But if you are not a Christian you should change one word. Change the word "you" into "I". There's a door that is open and "I" may go in ... when "I" come as a sinner to Jesus.'

So the pianist struck up the opening chords, and everybody sang lustily – except Rona. She knew she could not sing the last line, about coming as a sinner to Jesus. She didn't feel she was a sinner. She might not be perfect, but she certainly did not think she was a sinner. Yet that was what the speaker had explained was the basis on which one first came to Jesus, and then committed one's life to him ...

'I went away quietly after that meeting and really struggled with this and thought it through on my own. And eventually I said, "Lord, yes, I do admit that I am a sinner and I do believe Jesus died for me", and then I asked Christ into my life. I said, "Please come in and take control". It was as simple as that.'

It was followed by no ecstatic experience, nor any apparent change in her manner of life. She was just quietly settled in her own mind, but felt the next day that she should tell Jeanette what had happened. Jeanette looked at her and then said quietly,

'It's what I have been praying would happen. I've been praying for you all ever since I started teaching in the school.'

For Jeanette the Ambassador House Party in 1961 was the crowning event of her teaching assignment at Chorleywood College. Not only Rona, but two of the other girls she had brought came to saving faith in Christ at that house party. It seemed like a reassuring seal that God had indeed called her to serve him among the blind, and a month later she was starting her Bible College training in preparation for a lifetime of such work in India.

For Rona it was very different. Her ambition to live in the work-a-day world of ordinary sighted people was leading her into the most desolate period of her life. Several applications to enter teachers' training colleges had been refused on the grounds of her blindness until the welcome letter had come from the Principal of Saffron Walden that a place would be found for her there. And now, a month after the house party, here she was discovering for the first time how hard it is to be blind.

2

Teacher Training

There is no doubt that the Principal of Saffron Walden Teachers' Training College did the best she could for Rona. That she had even accepted her as a student was a great concession, for there were no facilities in the college for blind students. Arrangements were made for Rona to have her study-bedroom on the ground floor, so that she would not have so far to go to lectures and the dining room, she was allowed to have a tape recorder for lectures and make notes in braille, and to type rather than write her exercises. A rough idea of the lay-out of the college was explained to her, and times for meals and lectures – and after that she must fit into college life as best she could, among 170 others who were also students, fifty or more of them new arrivals like herself, and strangers in Saffron Walden.

The only difference between her and the others was that they could all see – see each other, see the corridors and staircases, see the classrooms into which they went, see the lecturer and what he was demonstrating, see when there was a new notice on the board ... Only she had to find her way sightlessly around, to learn what was going on by listening attentively to announcements or conversations, to sense the presence of someone who was sitting or standing soundlessly around.

None of the other students had had any close connection with a blind person before, and did not know how to react when they met her. When they saw her coming it was instinctive to stand quietly aside so as not to impede her progress, stop talking momentarily when they suddenly realized she had entered the room and could not see them, make rather embarrassed efforts to help her when she seemed in danger of tripping over something. She soon became conscious that they regarded her as different – almost an oddity. She knew no-one there, so was without one person whose voice she could recognize and to whom she could turn. She was always reluctant to ask for help, with the result that it took her over a week even to find her way around the college, recognize the different lecture rooms and libraries, and know where each lecture would be held. She always tried to go along with others to the lectures, for she was afraid of arriving late and causing a disturbance by fumbling around for an empty desk.

Finding an empty place at the dining room table was often a difficulty, but what she dreaded more than anything else was the weekends when there were what were called 'free meals'. It was a simple enough arrangement whereby the students went along at the time that suited them, helped themselves to whatever they liked on the sideboard, then sat to eat it at one of the dining tables. For Rona it meant entering the room without seeing whether anyone else was there, being alert for any sounds that would guide her, sensing by smell what food was on the sideboard, where it was placed – whether she would need a spoon or a fork to put it on her plate – and then feeling her way with it to find an empty seat, without bumping into anything or anyone.

It was so much easier when everyone sat down together and plates were passed along the table!

She dreaded the weekends.

The only thing that she found easy during that first term was the two weeks teaching practice that was included in the curriculum. Perhaps unknown to her the Principal had made a special selection of the village school to which she should go. Certainly the headmistress there was really supportive, and had prepared the children so well that they revealed not the slightest surprise that the new teacher could not see. And it soon became apparent that Rona was what is known as 'a born teacher'. Right from the start she had the children's attention and right from the start she was conscious of loving them. It was the only bright period in the whole of the first term, but it was not sufficient to reassure her that she could go through three years of this lonely strain. Lying in the bath one evening, trying to relax in the warm water, she gave expression to her feelings in a sort of conversation with herself.

'It's all too hard for you', she said. 'I'm just wasting my time – I can't go through with it.' Then she added, 'I don't even know whether I believe in God or not'.

It was at this point, approaching despair, that something happened which she always referred to as God coming to her and speaking to her. She heard no voice, saw no vision, but thoughts filled her mind so powerfully and convincingly that she did not doubt who had spoken.

'Yes, I am here. I had my hand on your life even before you became a Christian. And don't forget I brought you to the Training College although you weren't really aware of me, didn't consult me. But I brought you here, and I am with you here. Just talk to me about things, and I will help you.'

It made a difference. She started to pray about the loneliness, the strangeness, the difficulty of studying the reference books in the library. She could not read them even when she held them close to her eyes and squinted, for the print was too small, and of course there were no books in braille. Unless someone read aloud to her, how would she do the necessary study?

God usually works almost imperceptibly, sometimes through a simple act that sets in motion a string of events leading to circumstances and relationships that might otherwise not occur. In Rona's case it was Jeanette Short who proved the catalyst. She was concerned about the spiritual welfare of her erstwhile pupil, and took the practical step of finding out whether there was a Christian Union at the Teachers' Training College in Saffron Walden. Having learned that there was one, a letter was written to the leader of the Union, telling her about Rona.

Nothing else was needed. The members of the Christian Union, most of whom were in their second or third year of training, alerted to the fact that the blind student in the first year group was a Christian, sought her out to see what they could do to help her. Although studying hard themselves, one or another would spare time to find the book she needed and read quietly to her in the library, or in her own room.

They went further than that. What did she do on Saturdays, they enquired. When they found she had no appointments, they asked her if she would like to come with them on the bus into Cambridge. An organization there called Cambridge Inter College Christian Union – C.I.C.C.U. for short! – held special meetings on Saturday evenings in the Union Building. Rousing hymn-singing, prayer, and really good Bible teaching, with people like John Stott, Alec Motyer, David Watson and others coming to speak! If Rona would like to join them . . .?

If Rona would like to join them! Saturdays that had been so lonely and empty were transformed now. The chores like washing clothes, tidying drawers, shopping, all the domestic jobs that had to be done at the weekends were performed with the knowledge that at the end of the day there was the visit to Cambridge to look forward to. She would be going just as one of a group, like everyone else, to a church full of young people singing, praying, and listening eagerly to explanations of Bible passages the like of which she had never heard before.

It was all new to her, and so different from the formal church services she had always attended. Being handicapped visually was more of an asset than a liability in those meetings, for there was nothing to distract her, and she was able to give her whole-hearted attention to what she was hearing, storing away in her memory portions of Scripture that linked with others, elucidating or confirming the particular revelation or aspect of theology with which the speaker was dealing. She began to realize that the new life she had received on that memorable day when she had come, as a sinner, to Jesus, was being nourished and fed. Spiritually she was being satisfied.

But there was something else she longed for, although she would have hesitated to put it into words. It was a very natural longing, shared by all the human family. She just wanted friendship — personal friendship. It was something she had always had at Wavertree and then at Chorleywood, but somehow it seemed to be lacking here. Although there were now members of the Christian Union who were kind to her, willing to help her, who took her with them to the C.I.C.C.U. meetings on Saturday evenings, Sundays were usually rather lonely days for her. She went to church, where often enough there were people who knew her, sat beside her, occasionally whispered an explanation of something going on that she could not see, but after the service was over a cordial, 'Well, goodbye, Rona – see you again next week', meant going back to the college with the prospect of spending the rest of the day in her room.

All that changed after she met the Browns.

George and Margaret Brown belonged to a Brethren Assembly, so Rona, being an Anglican, might never have met them had it not been that one of the Christian Union members said to her one day,

'Rona, if you're not doing anything on Sunday afternoon, would you like to come to tea with the Browns? They're a very friendly couple, and keep open house for students – I know you'd be welcome.' So the next Sunday afternoon found her sitting at a crowded dining room table in a semi-detached house in a residential road in Saffron Walden, joining in the animated conversation that was punctuated by bursts of laughter as young people relaxed in the homely atmosphere of the Browns' household.

'Come and sit beside me while I'm pouring tea', her hostess said to Rona. 'Then we can get to know each other.' So started a friendship that enriched her life for the rest of the time she was in the Teachers' Training College.

Margaret Brown seemed to know instinctively what would make things easier for one who could not see. 'Here, Rona, try one of these scones', she said, pushing the plate towards her, so that she knew where it was and what was on it. 'Rona, I want you to have a piece of this cake before it's all gone!' And as everyone was leaving she made a special point of impressing on Rona that she'd be expecting to see her in good time for tea next Sunday.

So it became a regular item on her programme — tea on Sunday with the Browns. Nor did it stop there. Margaret soon learned of Rona's difficulty regarding reading the text books and her reluctance to ask for the help of fellow students who were themselves finding the study hard going, and made a suggestion.

'Bring them round to me one afternoon, and I'll read them to you.' It started with one afternoon a week, but it soon became three or even four, and often the session was concluded with an invitation to stay for tea. There might be only bread and butter and jam — all the cake having been eaten up on Sunday — but what did that matter? She was a welcome guest in a home with three cheerful school children, a home where she was soon accepted, understood and felt at ease. Here she could talk freely and be herself in a way that never seemed possible at college, where her visual handicap put her in a different category from the other students, robbing her of her self confidence.

The Browns' hospitable home made more impression on Rona than anything else. Unknown to her at the time, it was preparation for what lay ahead, where the simple opening of her home was to play so important a part in her life. At the time there was no prospect of her having a home of her own and all she could do, thinking it over, was to make a solemn promise to God that if ever she had one, she would be hospitable.

As things turned out, she had her first opportunity to fulfil that promise much sooner than she had anticipated. All the students, at the end of their first year of training, moved from the college into accommodation outside, and Rona wanted to do the same. Not unnaturally, the Principal refused, saying that she must remain in her room on the ground floor. It would be much safer for her there – the Principal was not willing to take the responsibility of having her live outside.

Rona admitted later that she was 'rather peeved' about this. Once again she was made to feel different from the others. Surely she had proved, after a year in college, that she was capable of looking after herself! She had done all her own chores, found her way to the shops, the bus station, done all the usual things without bothering anyone. She was quite capable of sharing a flat outside college, like the other girls. She kept her irritation to herself, but it was there until a thought entered her mind which quietened her. Perhaps there was a purpose in her being in that room on the ground floor. Perhaps there was something she could do to help the new girls coming to the college – invite them in, tell them things that might be useful to know, make them feel there was someone they could turn to, a door they could knock on and be sure of a welcome. And it was somewhere where the girls who were living out could always leave their coats if they wanted to.

She had made the vow to be hospitable if ever she had a home of her own. This was the place to start.

There in the study bedroom in the Teachers' Training College was laid the foundation of an indispensable part of the effectiveness of her future life. There she learned to turn aside from anything that had been occupying her attention, however important, as though it did not matter, in order to put a visitor completely at ease. There she learned to listen as well as talk – and the kettle was always handy to make a cup of tea. It became quite natural to 'Pop in and see Rona'. Even the matron went there from time to time, though for a different reason.

'When I'm showing visitors around and want them to see a study-bedroom, I always take them into yours,' she said. 'You see, I know it will always be tidy.'

Although being practically blind put certain limitations on Rona as a teacher, there was one way in which it actually proved an asset. An inspector, talking to all the young trainees after attending classes in which they were teaching, asked them, 'Which one of you can see what each child is doing in a class of about forty? Do you know when one or two of them are quietly squabbling, or playing up in one way or another?' A significant silence followed his question, and he continued, 'You can't see all of them at the same moment, so you need to become aware of atmosphere – develop intuition, a sort of sixth sense . . .' Then he added rather surprisingly, 'Miss Waller already has it.'

3

Learning God's Will

Job hunting can be a frustrating even rather humiliating experience for young people who have successfully completed an academic course and now feel ready to launch out into life. High expectations are not always realized, and although Rona had obtained her Teacher's Diploma with good marks she was prepared for difficulties in view of her obvious handicap. She answered several advertisements for infant teachers in the area around Faversham in Kent, where her parents were living, and set off for her first interview with much prayer and some trepidation.

Her first interview proved to be her last. It went off so well she could scarcely believe it. Perhaps her references had worked in her favour more than she realized. To her amazement she was offered the position of teacher in the Milton Regis Infants School near Sittingbourne, to start work in September.

So commenced a very happy period in her life. The work was heavy, with a class of forty-three children aged between four and a half and seven, and there were times when she returned home feeling quite exhausted. But she loved the children, and had no problems in keeping control. They were divided into what was called family groups, according not only to age but also ability, and this method suited her better than having them all together. The other teachers were friendly and helpful, and as she had joined a Baptist church in Faversham where there was a group of young people about the same age as herself, life was very congenial.

Her desire to live among sighted people as one of themselves was being satisfied. Although she could not play games like tennis or badminton, she could sit with the onlookers and join in as they chatted, cheer the winners, encourage the losers, and she was always quick to produce cold drinks for over-heated players. She was thoroughly at home in the church kitchen where she ensured that there was always an adequate supply of tea and sugar, milk and biscuits. There were certain roles into which she fitted and found a niche, so that she was missed if she was not there. Bible classes were easy, providing she knew beforehand what book would be studied so that she could borrow a braille edition and take it along with her. But with the book to be studied on her knees she could find the chapter and verse called for as quickly as anyone. Her forefinger slid rapidly over the embossed dots, and she joined in the discussions eagerly.

She took to heart the emphasis laid by the church leaders on the importance of prayer in the life of a Christian – prayer not only for oneself and one's personal relationships, but prayer for others, including those who were serving God overseas. The seeds of interest in India had been sown by Jeanette Short, who was already in that country as a member of the Bible and Medical Missionary Fellowship*. Jeanette's experience of teaching blind students in Chorleywood led naturally to her working among blind people, and she was being seconded to the Sharp Memorial School for the Blind in Rajpur, north India.

The history of the Sharp Memorial School for the Blind went back over a hundred years, when a little girl in England contracted measles and lost her sight. She was blind for over a year, but eventually recovered, and then she made a vow. All through life she would try to help blind people, whenever and wherever possible. It was a vow she never forgot, and when she went to India as a missionary she soon learned something of the plight of blind people in that country. She saw beggars, sightlessly holding out empty up-turned hands, into which an occasional alms was thrown – not out of compassion, but that the donor might 'gain merit'. She heard of little girls taken into the temples for a life of prostitution. She soon discovered how deep and how widespread was the social effect of Hinduism. Belief in reincarna-

---

* Now known as Interserve.

tion and the power of implacable deities led to indifference to the suffering of others. Suffering? There was a reason for it. Misfortune and handicap in this life was due to wrong doing in one's previous existence. It was Karma, the will of the gods. Nothing could be done about it. Giving birth to a blind baby, and the blindness itself came into this category, and therefore must be endured without any help from others. The only hope for the sufferer was to gain enough merit by offerings and pilgrimages to temples, by self-inflicted wounds, or by some other means, to obtain a better re-birth after death, and so improve one's position in the never-ending cycle of life.

The young missionary thought about the matter, prayed about it, made various enquiries and decided the best way to help would be to provide a school where blind girls could be taught skills that would enable them to support themselves. She shared this idea with Annie Sharp, a friend in England, who took special training for such work before going to India herself. On her arrival arrangements were made for an industrial home for blind girls to be established on the compound of St. Catherine's Hospital in Amritsar.

So was started in 1887 what came to be known as the Sharp Memorial School for the Blind. It was the first of its kind in the whole of India. Until that time, even in Christian communities, nothing had been done to help or encourage blind people. Even if they were allowed into church to listen, they were more or less shunned and left to themselves. In most cases they never got as far as to a church. Their parents, ashamed of having a blind child, kept them out of sight at home. Not surprisingly, many of them died when young . . .

By 1965 much more practical help was being given to blind people, yet places in the specialized schools and colleges were totally inadequate to cater for a million blind children needing education. The Sharp Memorial School, situated now in the foothills of the Himalayas, had a nation-wide reputation in the scattered churches and mission centres. It was known as a Christian school for girls and small boys, irrespective of creed or class.

To this school, after a period of language study, Jeanette had been seconded, but she remained a member of BMMF. Consequently Rona, who received their magazines and books, found her interest widening to other countries where the society had workers. Afghanistan in particular, attracted her attention. In one of the meetings in the Faversham church a missionary who had been living on the border of the country had painted such a vivid picture of the remote, mountainous regions, the horsemen whirling across the plains, the Pathan tribesmen, the veiled women, above all the need for the gospel, that she began to wonder if she should go there herself. The country was cautiously opening its doors to western aid missions, and as workers with families of their own moved in she might go too, as an infant teacher to ex-patriate children.

That she might use her skills and experience to teach in the Sharp Memorial School for the Blind

never occurred to her. The idea simply did not cross
her mind. She wanted to do what she could to help
forward the work of God somewhere in Asia, but
among sighted people, not among those who were
handicapped visually. However, in those early years
of teaching in the Sittingbourne area her mind was
fully occupied with her immediate circumstances, for
during her second term in the Milton Regis School
she took a step which she later realized was a
mistake. A well-meaning friend told her of a situation that would be vacant in the next academic year
in a village school with a class of children not
exceeding thirty. How much easier it would be for
her to teach a class of that size than the one she had
now, of over forty! The salary would be the same,
travelling would be equally easy, and it would be so
much less exhausting.

Rona agreed promptly. It seemed a sensible move
to make. It would leave her less tired at the end of
the day, she would have more time for church
activities and to help her mother at home. In every
way the prospect was appealing. She applied for the
job and was accepted, gave notice that she would be
leaving Milton Regis school at the end of the school
year – and then she began to have misgivings. She
would be a stranger at the school to which she was
going, while here at Milton Regis she knew everyone.
All the other teachers accepted her disability as
though it did not exist, the children's parents would
greet her cheerily when they met her by saying
'Hello! This is Mary's Dad,' or 'This is Sidney's
Mum'. She was in a happy environment where she

felt thoroughly at ease, and into which she had every reason to believe God had guided her. Now she had unwittingly taken matters into her own hands. She had not consulted God about it – it had seemed so obviously a wise thing to do, and she had just gone ahead and taken steps from which she could not withdraw.

When September came, and she started at the new school, she found that her misgivings were not ill-founded. She knew none of the teachers, and as they were all older than she and well established, she was uncomfortably aware of being an object of some curiosity and speculation. The children were mildly curious, and she heard them telling their parents 'our teacher can't see'. Worst of all, the headmistress had the disconcerting habit of coming unannounced to the door of the classroom where she was teaching, flinging it open, and shouting if she noticed anything with which she could find fault. One incident left an indelible impression on Rona's memory. She was explaining something to the children, who seemed to be listening attentively, when suddenly the door clicked open and the familiar voiced yelled,

'Why has James got paint in his hair?' Rona had no answer to give, for of course she could not see the offending paint, nor know how it had got there. It served only to undermine her authority over the children, and accentuate her consciousness of her own inadequacy.

Looking back over that period in her life, she had to admit that she had made a mistake – and it taught her a lesson. Never again would she take an important step in life, however practical it seemed, without praying about it, and genuinely waiting for God's confirmation that it was right. Yet even now, though she was suffering mentally as her confidence was being undermined, she learned that God had not forsaken her. She was comforted, as so often happens, through a fellow human being. In this case it was the other infant teacher, to whom she confided her fear that because she could not see to correct the children's writing, their work would be poor.

'Don't worry about that,' said Jean reassuringly. 'I can soon correct what they have done, and show them how to put it right. And you're so good on the other subjects you teach them. The right answers they give to questions, their number work, their spelling, their action play, the way they memorize! It all shows they've had a good teacher. Don't worry about their writing!' And so her confidence as a teacher was restored, while church activities among older children presented no problems. She taught a Sunday School class, the children arriving and greeting 'Miss Waller' as eagerly and naturally as anyone else.

In this sphere of her life things went naturally enough in another way, too. She fitted in happily with the other young people of her own age, male as well as female, and she began to find herself specially drawn to one young man who hoped to train for the Christian ministry. She was still interested in Jeanette Short's work, and that of other branches of Interserve, and sent money regularly towards their support. She wanted to be in what is termed 'full-time

Christian service' herself – but increasingly the desire
was linked with Alan. She wanted to be in it with
him. Quite unconsciously she was drifting – in the
wrong direction.

She was brought to an abrupt halt one Sunday
evening at church. The preacher was not even an
ordained clergyman, only a lay preacher, but he was
God's messenger to Rona. He chose as his Bible
reading verses 57–62 in Luke's Gospel, chapter nine,
and he spoke on 'Would-be Followers Of Jesus'.
There was the man who was willing to follow him –
but not until he had gone to bury his father. There
was the one who wanted to go home first and say
goodbye to all his family, and THEN follow Jesus.

'In fact, they had their conditions. They were
willing to follow him, providing they could do it in
their own way, and in their own time. Have you got
conditions about following Jesus . . . ?'

That was the gist of the preacher's sermon that
night, and if it affected no-one else, it affected Rona.
'I realized that I was putting a condition that I would
do anything for the Lord – but let me have Alan to
do it with . . .' That was her condition.

She walked back from church that evening in a
very sobered frame of mind, and went straight to
bed. But she couldn't sleep. She tossed and turned,
wanting to forget everything, but sleep eluded her,
and she knew why. She had to get this matter settled.
So she got out of bed and knelt beside it, admitted
she had had conditions about discipleship, but now,

'Lord, what do you want me to do?' she prayed.
The words that flooded her mind in answer to that

prayer were totally unexpected, and in a way seemed so unreasonable that she questioned them.

'Apply to the London Bible College', were the words. Apply to the London Bible College? Surely that was not meant for her?

'But Lord, the London Bible College is for academic people. I wouldn't be clever enough. I'm only an infant teacher . . .' She must have been mistaken in what she thought the Lord was saying to her, she decided, and got back into bed. She did not even know the address of the London Bible College. In any case, she would be quite unsuitable . . .

She did nothing about it on Monday, trying to dismiss the words from her mind, but by Tuesday she was so uneasy she knew she must do something. She found the address of the London Bible College, which at that time was near Baker Street in central London, and wrote for an application form.

After that, things moved quickly. She was invited to go for an interview, was accepted for a London University two-year diploma course in theology, arranged to share a flat with a friend rather than live in the hall of residence, and in the autumn of 1967 again found herself a student, but in surroundings where she felt completely at home.

4

London Bible College

Edyth Banks was one of the students at LBC and riding there on the back of her scooter from Wandsworth Common to the College was fun, especially going round Hyde Park Corner and Marble Arch. Rona thoroughly enjoyed it. Some people thought it was rather dangerous, but if Edyth herself was prepared to take the risk, she certainly was. She didn't mention it to her parents, though, at least not for the first six months. By that time they had met Edyth and said they were sure she wasn't the type to do anything risky, so they weren't worried. In any case, it happened only twice a week. The other days one of the lecturers, Tim Buckley, who lived nearby with his wife and family, took her there in his ten-seater van.

It was one of the College jokes that Rona's methods of arriving each day ranged from the ridiculous to the sublime.

She was sharing a flat with a teacher whom she knew and was fulfilling her long-felt desire to be living just like other young women of her age. Shopping presented no problems. She enjoyed housekeeping and cooking, and was even able to do some entertaining, inviting friends for lunch or early supper at weekends. A local church, Trinity Road Chapel, was within walking distance, so she went there on Sundays when she was not in Faversham, and altogether life was so full and satisfying that she soon forgot about Alan.

Settling into London Bible College was so different from her experiences at training college. Here people were so friendly, accepting her as one of themselves. Right from the start fellow students sought her out, introducing themselves, then greeting her whenever they saw her coming towards them.

'Hello Rona! This is Graham . . .' or 'Hello Rona, this is Mary . . .' so that she soon learned to recognize them by their voices, and even by their footsteps. Not all were English. 'Hello Rona, this is Daniel Abrahams' was spoken clearly, but with a slight accent. She later learned he was from India. They all offered to help her in any way they could. To read aloud to her from the books they were studying would be no problem, they assured her – they had to read the material anyhow, and she had to as well – so why not read it together? One and another came alongside in this way with the consequence that her programme at college was always full. Although the course was, she admitted, academically tough, the notes she made in braille were adequate, and at the end of her first term she packed them all up carefully and posted them by braille free post to her parents' home in Faversham, to study during the holiday.

But they never arrived.

She waited for several days for them to be delivered, then went to the Post Office to make enquiries, and was told no braille parcels had been received for Miss Rona Waller. Further enquiries, phone calls, letters written by friends, all proved fruitless. Those heavy parcels of notes in braille, so carefully prepared and posted, had apparently vanished into thin air. They were never discovered.

It was a serious setback in her study, and although eventually she got help from the Students' Library for the Blind, which re-brailled some of the official college notes for her, this could not make up for the time that had been lost. Philosophy was her weakest subject. She failed completely in that, which meant she did not obtain the first part of her diploma, and would have to spend an extra year in college. It proved a very practical exercise in what is known as accepting disappointments philosophically!

During her second year at LBC Rona started applying to BMMF to become one of its missionaries like Jeanette Short. There was one country in particular where she believed she could make a useful contribution through the team of Christians that was starting to work there. The International Assistance Mission was providing practical help in Afghanistan, a country that had been cut off from many aspects of modern technology, and one branch of its activities was a school for the blind. As a qualified and experienced teacher she would have a role to play, and her visual handicap could even prove to be an advantage. It would provide tangible evidence of what can be accomplished by blind people.

It was an almost unheard-of thing for a blind person to offer for service with BMMF, or any other such organization, but her application was not turned down. In any case, no decision could be taken until she had completed her course and obtained the Diploma in Theology.

It is doubtful whether anyone at BMMF knew just what it had cost her to make the offer. She had wanted to be a missionary, to work for God overseas, but she had taken it for granted it could be among sighted people. She felt totally integrated in the ordinary work-a-day world, and had neither desire for or thought of living among blind people again. What appeared to be a casual conversation had suddenly confronted her with the realization that she was choosing her own path from completely selfish motives.

She was talking to the occupant of another flat in the same house where she was living, and had been relating some of her own experiences, especially those that had led to her becoming a Christian. Then she mentioned that she hoped to go to Afghanistan as a missionary.

'So I suppose you'll go to work among blind people?' her neighbour remarked. Rona's reply was swift and definite.

'Oh no. No! I'll go to teach in an ordinary school – not among the blind.' She spoke vehemently. 'Not among blind people.'

'Well, well!' was the rather scornful rejoinder. 'You talk about Christianity meaning a lot to you, and how sighted people came to your blind school and told you about Christ, and how they were willing to take you and those other blind girls to camp and all that ... yet you won't go to tell other blind people about Jesus, who is supposed to be real to you.' She shrugged her shoulders and turned away.

Rona was speechless. The words had obviously been spoken without any premeditation, and they came as a shock to her, but as she descended the stairs and re-entered her flat, she knew she could not brush them away. However brusquely they had been spoken there was truth in what they implied. Once again in the quietness of her own room, she yielded reluctantly to what she did not want to acknowledge. This time it was that her visual handicap put her in the category of blind people, and as such it was to be expected that she would reach out to help others similarly afflicted. This might even be the purpose of God himself regarding her – yet here she was, deliberately planning her life apart from blind people, planning to avoid them. As she thought about it she came to the conclusion that the Lord had used those piercing words to speak to her. She had deserved them.

After that experience she was prepared to go to work in the blind school in Afghanistan. She'd be able to teach them to read braille. Without that they would go all their lifetimes without ever reading anything. Even if the Bible were translated into their own language they would not be able to read it, unless it were produced for them in braille.

To be unable to read the Word of God! She thought of what it meant to her to open one of her precious books and run her fingers over familiar passages, reassuring herself that they were meant for her, for her personally.

'Let not your heart be troubled: ye believe in God, believe also in me. In my Father's house are many mansions: if it were not so, I would have told you. I go to prepare a place for you. And if I go and prepare a place for you, I will come again, and receive you unto myself; that where I am, there ye may be also . . .'

Or . . .

'Search the Scriptures; for in them ye think ye have eternal life: and they are they which testify of me. . .'

Or the heartening story of the man who had been born blind.

'. . . Master, who did sin, this man, or his parents, that he was born blind? Jesus answered, Neither hath this man sinned, nor his parents: but that the works of God should be made manifest in him . . .' That story was particularly prized. There was a PURPOSE in having been born blind – that the works of God should be made manifest.

Rona had not many of the books of the Bible in her personal possession. There simply was not room for the sixty-six volumes on the shelves in her room.

She had been in the habit of borrowing from the Students' Library for the Blind any book which she specially wanted to study. But there were just a few which were her own, and for which she always found room. The gospel of John was one of them.

But blind people in Afghanistan hadn't even got that . . . So Rona started making her application to go there with BMMF.

'Lord, if it's not your will, please close the door', she prayed, but she did not expect him to do so. She believed it was the way she should go, and tried to find out all she could about the country and its people. Her studies at LBC were going well, too, and everything seemed to be leading in the direction of a missionary career, when suddenly she began to have pain in her back. She had suffered with it before, but it had given no trouble for years – now the pain became acute. She saw the doctor, then the specialist, her condition was diagnosed as being 'a slipped disc' and rather than operate it was decided she should go for a course of treatment and rest into St. James Hospital. It was an alarming situation. How could she continue her studies, lying on her back in a hospital ward? She had already been put back a year by the loss of those brailled notes earlier.

Friends came to her rescue. Edyth had completed her own course at LBC and was working for the United Bible Societies, but she was able to fit in a visit to see Rona each afternoon, read to her or bring fresh material for her to study. After she left, Winifred Urech, the lady worker of Trinity Road Chapel, came along to continue reading to her, so the problem of how to keep up with her studies was solved. And once again her visual handicap proved an asset after it was 'lights out' in the ward. There was nothing to hinder her from reading under the bed-clothes. She needed no light.

That spell in St. James Hospital brought her to a condition nearer to despair than she had ever known. How could she go back to teaching, with the need to be standing for hours every day? And what else would there be for her to do?

The door to working among blind people in Afghanistan was closed. A member of the staff of BMMF had visited her specially to explain, as gently as possible, that there could be no thought of considering her application until she had had a clean bill of health for at least two years. It was not her visual handicap that was the obstacle, it was quickly added, but the risk of sending anyone out whose physical condition was a hazard.

Yes, Rona nodded, she quite understood. It could be weeks, if not months, before she would be fit enough to leave hospital, anyway. She gave no indication of how numb she felt at the confirmation of what she had begun to suspect was the closing of the door to Afghanistan. As she admitted years later, 'It was a time when I was very, very low. I had prayed that if it wasn't right, that God would close the door, but I must admit I never for one moment thought he would . . . I was very, very low.' Lying on her back in the hospital ward, still studying as best she could for the exams on which so much depended as far as obtaining a Diploma of Theology was concerned, it was the hardest struggle she had known. Edyth continued visiting her each afternoon, and this helped a lot, since she knew the Course and could guide her – and encourage her, too.

There came a day, however, when Edyth did not arrive. She would not be free this afternoon, she had explained, but instead sent a little card on which she had scribbled a verse from Jeremiah chapter 29.

'I have plans for you', says the Lord. 'Plans for good and not for evil. I will give you a future and a hope.'

Holding the card close to her eyes Rona was able to distinguish the words, and everything seemed to recede as they sank into her mind. The busy ward, the nurses moving along with trolleys, the thought of the study she ought to be doing, the fear of what would be the result of her time in hospital, and what the future might hold of emptiness and pain . . . all were subdued under the quiet authority of those words.

'I have plans – for you. Plans for good . . . a future and a hope.' Just the words, and the conviction that they came from God.

A few days later she received a letter asking if she would be willing to mark replies sent in to the London Bible College Braille Correspondence Course run by Torch Trust for the Blind. This was obviously something she was qualified to do, but it would involve her visiting the Trust which was situated in Hurstpierpoint, in Sussex.

Meanwhile, the treatment and rest in hospital had proved ineffective as far as the slipped discs were concerned, so another method was tried. Rona was put into a plaster cast from neck to the bottom of her spine, and discharged from hospital, to return to as normal a life as possible in the circumstances. To do her shopping, cooking and household chores in addition to her study was obviously too much for her, and Edyth's vicar and his wife came up with a suggestion.

'Let her come and live with us for a few weeks,' they said. 'One extra won't make any difference!' They already had a growing family, and it would not be difficult to change bedrooms around to accommodate a guest. So into the hospitable Hall household she went, and with Tim Buckley to give her a lift to LBC when necessary, she managed to keep up with her studies.

She was still in a plaster cast, and would be for some weeks to come. How was she to visit Torch Trust for the Blind? Again Edyth came to solve the problem.

'I'll take you down there on Whit Monday', she said, adding that she wouldn't go on her scooter – she now had her Mother's old car! So to Torch Trust for the Blind they went for the day, and Rona had her introduction to the place and the work that was to play so significant a part in her life.

5

Introduction to the Torch Trust

At the time when Rona visited it, Torch Trust for the Blind was already a well established organization devoted to producing Christian literature in braille. Ronald and Stella Heath, founders and leaders of the work were away, but two members of the committee were there to welcome her, and on entering the large, sprawling house she was surprised to find herself feeling quite at home. It was light and airy, she knew that, and as she was shown round she could sense, though she couldn't see, the vast open views of Sussex trees, fields and rolling hills, visible through the windows. There were some bedrooms on the ground floor, besides the main rooms, she was told, and one great advantage was that the whole area was on one level – no awkward little steps to trip up the forgetful and unseeing, or visitors coming for the first time.

There were always visitors coming for the first time, she learned, for Torch House, as it was called, seemed to have ever open doors for blind people, especially those who were lonely. Ron and Stella were evidently addicted to hospitality. In fact, the work in which they, as well as other members of staff were now engaged full time, had started in their home in Reigate where, though they had a family of four children, they managed to fit in a club for teenage girls every Friday evening.

The club was a cheerful affair. The girls were made to feel thoroughly at home, and spent their time sewing, knitting, 'messing about with plaster moulds', and chatting. But there was more to it than that. Every evening ended with an epilogue, and what they heard in those short talks brought some of those girls to personal faith in the Lord Jesus Christ.

One of them worked as a cook in a Training Centre run by the Royal National Institute for the Blind, and one Friday evening, as she was leaving, she asked Stella Heath, 'Can I bring a blind girl to the club next week?'

'Yes, I should think so', was the rather absent-minded answer. Stella was thinking of something else. There had never been a blind girl in the club before, but the addition of one could make little difference, so next Friday evening Wendy came. She seemed to have no desire to do anything. Handwork was evidently not in her line. She was just content to sit rather listlessly, listening to what was going on, though when the time came for a sing-song she joined in with enthusiasm. But the epilogue really fastened her attention, and Friday after Friday she listened, noticed how some of the girls talked about

Jesus as though they knew and loved him, and eventually responded to the simple suggestion made by one of the girls that she should ask him into her heart. The following day she went to see Stella and told her, 'I know he is my Friend now.'

The change in her after that was marked – so marked that not only had Stella noticed it, but also the Principal of the Training Centre. Wendy, who had been so hard to teach, so lacking in confidence, so lethargic, had become alive, eager to learn, responsive to encouragement to such an extent that he told the Heaths, 'Since coming to you she has changed so much that we shall now be able to train her for a job.' She had almost been written off as a hopeless case before. Then he turned to them and said, 'There are twenty-five others here. Can you help them as well?'

Twenty-five others – and some of them were boys. All of them were visually handicapped, so they would not really fit into the Friday evening club anyway. So the Heaths started inviting boys as well as girls from the Training Centre to come to tea on Sunday afternoon – that gave the opportunity to take them to church afterwards. Just as in the Friday club, so at the Sunday afternoon tea parties, some of the young people whose hearts had been touched by the kindness and hospitality shown, realized that Christ was the true source of it, and put their trust in him.

It did not end there for Ron and Stella. These young believers must be nurtured. It was easy enough while they were living locally, but few of them remained long at the Training Centre, and how would they fare when they left to take up jobs for which they had been trained? Probably with no Christian fellowship.

'We must keep in touch with them somehow", the Heaths said to each other. "Encourage them . . . Help them in their Christian lives . . .'

The only way to do it would be to write to them – and that must be in braille. So they learned enough braille to enable them to write simple letters. It was the best they could do – they wished it could be better. Then they heard about Torch.

Torch was a Christian magazine in braille. A Christian magazine in braille! How wonderful! It was very small in one way, for each issue comprised only about 1,000 words, though they covered several sheets of embossed paper, making a booklet needing a huge envelope to be mailed to each reader. In some ways the magazine was rather old-fashioned, but it contained the gospel message and the Word of God, so the Heaths wrote to the editor, explaining what they were doing among young blind people, and asking for six copies of Torch to be sent to them regularly.

This was done for some time, and then the editor wrote to them. She was an old lady of eighty-two, and knew the time had come when she could continue the work no longer. If no-one else could take it on, it would have to cease, and the several hundreds of blind readers to whom it was sent every alternate month would receive it no more. The question she asked was, would they accept responsibility for editing Torch?

So that is how they started on what became a full-time occupation. They sometimes wondered, rather humorously, whether the Heaths had taken over Torch, or whether Torch had taken over the Heaths.

The editing and production of the little magazine opened up to them a vast field of unmet need. The old lady who had been responsible died within days of handing over, and the library of Christian books in braille she had accumulated was passed on to them. It was contained at first in what used to be called 'the butler's pantry'. So started the lending library, and it was increasingly impressed on Ron and Stella that there was a tremendous lack of Christian literature for the blind. More and more shelves were put up in their home, as braille Christian books were collected and transcribed. (A little shed they purchased became the first Torch property.) Their house in Reigate proved too small to accommodate the books and the equipment, as well as the visitors and helpers who came to them. They had to move into more suitable premises. At the age when they would normally have begun thinking about retirement they had entered their life-work.*

By the time Rona visited them for the first time they had already moved to the large house in

---

* The story of Torch Trust for the Blind is told in *Where There Is Vision* by Stella Heath, published by Marshall Pickering in conjunction with Torch Trust for the Blind.

Hurstpierpoint, from which braille leaflets, booklets, books were flowing out steadily all over the United Kingdom and beyond. When Rona went into the library she was amazed to find how many books were there. If only she had known! So many books that she would have loved to read in those years since she had become a Christian. As it was, there was one book she was able to take away with her. It was the Revised Standard Version of the Book of Daniel which she needed to study for her next exam at LBC.

However, more than the production of Christian literature in braille was going on at Torch House, Rona learned. House parties were held there from time to time, when blind people came for a holiday specially planned for them, with things going on which they could join – and with everything on the same level on the ground floor! Rona remembered the first house party to which she had gone, and what it had meant to her.

That first brief visit was followed a few weeks later by a longer one, when Rona met Stella Heath to talk over the work involved in the Correspondence Course.

'It's the first time I've interviewed anyone lying on their back', laughed Stella. During that interview Rona confided her reluctance to work with blind people – a reluctance that Stella herself had known when she found herself being drawn into it. The two got on well together, and after three days there Rona wondered if God had a purpose for her beyond what she had expected, in bringing her to Torch House.

She mentioned it to Stella, adding, 'But I don't know what else I could do, apart from the Correspondence Course. After all, I'm only an infant school teacher.'

Stella had a suggestion. She really needed help in writing and editing the magazine, she said, and if Rona could do this it would greatly lessen her burden of work. She gave Rona a series to work on, and it proved so satisfactory that she assured her there would certainly be something for her to do if she could spend more time in Torch House.

The summer of 1970, restricted as she was physically, was a significant period in her life. She had taken all her exams, lying on her back and dictating the answers to a secretary sent from London University. She passed, obtaining her Dip. Th. diploma. When the time came to go back into hospital it was discovered that the condition of the vertebrae had in no way improved. Her only hope now was to have the very delicate operation that the surgeon himself had been reluctant to perform, for fear it might result in permanent damage rather than relief. As it turned out the operation was a complete success, and she had no more pain in her back.

After two months' recuperation she took up a part-time teaching job in a school near to her flat, which she was therefore able to keep on, thus retaining the independence that she so much prized. For over a year she lived half the week in London, and the other half in Hurstpierpoint.

However, the time came when the volume of work at Torch House was increasing at such a rate that she knew she had reached the limit of what she could do there, unless she gave up teaching. Besides the demand for more and more braille literature, the popularity and effectiveness of the house-parties was so obvious that they had to be continued at any cost, and now a new opportunity was presenting itself. People who had already been alerted to the work of Torch House were offering to make it known more widely, so that Torch Fellowship Groups could be started in other places. This would involve workers travelling from Hurstpierpoint to cities far and near to help the setting up of these groups, and to encourage those who ran them. Rona was obviously one who was specially well qualified for this, as she realized, but it would involve more than giving up her teaching job. It would mean giving up her flat, with its carefully arranged furnishings and its cupboards where she knew just where to find things, the flat in which she was free to live in the way that suited her – and where there was plenty of room.

But she knew she must do it. 'This is the way, walk in it', was a text quoted at the Torch Thanksgiving, and it was God's message to her.

To obey was not easy. To give up her flat and return to living in a community, she admitted years later, 'was quite a struggle. I really enjoyed having my own home, with its independence.' Then she added with a smile, 'God must have a sense of humour, because when I had agreed to live at Torch House full time, as there wasn't much space it meant sharing a small bedroom with another girl. The verse that God gave me the night before I actually went to

live at Torch was "Lengthen thy cords and streng-
then thy stakes." That meant "expand yourself and
move into a bigger tent"!'

Far from expanding she seemed to be going into
reverse, moving from a roomy flat into half a small
bedroom. Then she went on to explain, 'But the sort
of expansion I was moving into was moving into a
much bigger job. I was quite involved in a very
exciting stage at Torch, when they were setting up
Torch fellowship groups around the country. I
remember going to Glasgow and Liverpool and other
places. And I had already got quite involved in the
London Torch Fellowship.' This was held in a small
hall in Earls' Court Road, and at the opening
meeting Rona was just about to give the secretary's
report when an unrehearsed incident occurred. A
guide dog suddenly left his master's side, and
running towards Rona put his two paws on her
shoulders and lovingly tried to lick her face. Such a
sign of approval from an unexpected source relieved
the meeting of any uncomfortable formality.

*   *   *

Rona had been living and working in Torch House
for about eighteen months when Tony Gibb first
appeared over the horizon of her life. He was
introduced to her as one of the many voluntary
workers who came to help for longer or shorter
periods. He had offered to come in for half a day
once a week, and his first job was to dictate Bible

Correspondence notes to Rona, who put them into braille.

Neither of them liked the job, nor did they like each other. As a successful business man he felt she was altogether too bossy a young woman, and she resented the way he wanted to take over administration. What she did not know at the time was that he was passing through the most traumatic period of his life. His wife had deserted him and was living with another man. The efforts of two Baptist ministers to persuade her to return to her husband had failed, and as a Christian himself he was reluctant to divorce her. Anxiety about the effect the whole situation would have on his two sons added to his distress. It was largely on their account that he refused to transfer to the head office in Holland of the firm for which he was working. The result of that refusal was that he was made redundant – on Christmas Eve.

It was an experience he could never forget. As he said years later, he was at his wits' end when one of his sons came into his bedroom and placed beside him the Scripture Union notes of the day. It was the keynote that caught his eye. It read, 'When you hit rock bottom, Christ is there.'

He certainly felt he had hit rock bottom. Financially he was in no difficulty, investments from his savings were bringing him in an adequate income. But what was he to do with his time? Empty hours and empty days lay ahead, just when he needed to have his mind occupied, and an outlet for his energy. One of the Baptist ministers who was standing by him through this difficult period made a wise suggestion. Why not do some voluntary work for Christian organizations who would appreciate the sort of help he could give, with his experience and expertise in electronic machines, and marketing generally.

Torch Trust for the Blind proved to be one of those organizations. The work they were doing appealed to Tony, and he was able to help them in business matters and production problems. As the months passed he spent more and more time in the office, realizing that his marriage had broken down irretrievably. On his 25th wedding anniversary, while out walking alone, it was almost with a feeling of relief that he sensed God telling him to divorce his wife. The end had come.

The relationship between him and Rona continued to be cool. There was what he termed a clash of personalities on the few occasions when they worked together, although he was beginning to be attracted by what he saw of Christlikeness in her life. He had even got to the point of telling himself that if ever he married again, he'd want to marry Rona, and no-one else.

Just about this time, unknown to him Rona had started to pray about her attitude towards him. She faced the fact that she did not like the man, and that it was wrong. To be living in the same community without having true Christian love for each other simply was not right, so she prayed that the Lord would give her love for Tony Gibb.

The answer came in a way she had neither expected nor desired. It was almost with dismay that it gradually began to dawn on her that not only did she love him, but that she was *in love with Tony Gibb*.

6

Marriage and Move to India

The courtship of Tony and Rona was fraught with difficulties, hinging on the controversial subject of re-marriage after divorce. Rona herself was very dubious as to whether it was right or not, and at first refused Tony's proposal on those grounds. When at last she was convinced that God had planned it, she received heartening encouragement from some of her friends, particularly Tim and Doreen Buckley. Even more surprising, the pastor of Trinity Road Chapel, which had contributed towards her support, when he heard the whole story, offered to marry them in his church. He and some other pastors had been meeting at Westminster Chapel to pray over and research the subject of re-marriage after divorce, he told them, and had come to the conclusion that in some cases it was in the will of God. So on December 4th, 1976, Tony and Rona were married, and went to live in Tony's flat on the sea front at Eastbourne.

For Rona it meant not only a home of her own, but for the first time in her life being in possession of the whole Bible in braille. There were sufficient shelves in the flat to accommodate all sixty-six volumes. She fingered them with great satisfaction, putting them in right order from Genesis to Revelation, along with some of her other prized possessions which she had kept stored in her parents' home.

For both Tony and Rona it was a period in which they had the opportunity to pause and take stock of their position. After several years of living in a closely-knit and very busy community they were alone together and with plenty of time on their hands. They immediately looked round for a church, and decided on a small but growing Free Church near their flat. They joined in all the church activities, and found particularly good friends in Martyn and Sue Relf. Martyn was a R.E. teacher, but Sue, with their two small children to look after, had given up her secretarial work and was living at home. Tony and Rona often went round to visit her, and confided their uncertainty concerning their future. They felt in a sort of limbo, although they were sure that God had work for them to do. But what was it? They were glad to be able to pray with her, not only about church matters, but about their own future.

Several months passed before any requests came for Tony's services, then three arrived about the same time. Two in particular stood out. One was from United World Mission, outlining some suggestions about setting up a braille unit in Korea, and continuing,

'We would be looking for a couple like you, who would be willing to give a long term commitment to the mission field ... so just know that the door is wide open if God should lay the 100,000 blind of Korea on your hearts ... we would be delighted to have you on the team.'

The other was from Jeanette Short in India. Christoffel Blindenmission, a German organization known as CBM, needed someone to set up a braille press in Madras, where she herself was living at the time. Wasn't this just the sort of job that Tony could do? India! Rona's heart seemed to give a quickened throb at the sound of the word. Wasn't it the very place she had been specially interested in, had thought at one time it was where she should go? Madras. She did not even know whereabouts in India Madras was situated until, holding a map close to her eyes, she moved it about until she discovered the name in the south-east, on the coast. She wanted to go to India. But in her daily Bible reading she had come to Ephesians, and in chapter five read the words, 'Wives, submit yourselves unto your own husbands, as unto the Lord. For the husband is the head ...'

As she related years later, 'God spoke to me and made it plain that the husband is the head of the house. I felt this was God saying to me, "I am going to let you know through Tony what is right." ' It was for him to decide where they should go, and she was quite prepared in her mind for it to be Korea.

The more she thought about the two openings, the more convinced she became that the Korean project would suit Tony the better, and as they talked about it she was careful to emphasize its good points.

To her surprise, he did not agree. He had just the kind of experience needed to set up a Christian braille department in India, he said, and that was the country in which there was so much need for it. It was to India he felt they should go. So it was decided, and Tony got down to making arrangements in his usual businesslike manner. There was something he believed to be of primary importance, and talking it all over with Sue Relf, he asked her, 'Will you be our Prayer Secretary?' He and Rona were preparing to embark on a course which was entirely new to both of them. Neither of them had been to India, they knew no Indian language, while climate, customs, even food would be strange to them. They could easily make mistakes – perhaps serious mistakes. And they would need to discern God's guidance as they went forward to the work.

'We really need prayer about all this', they said. 'We've got friends who we know will pray for us, but they'll need to be informed, kept up to date with what we are doing. If we sent you a letter every so often, could you duplicate it and send it round?' Yes, Sue was very happy to take on that responsibility, she assured them – and the time to start was now!

The Gibb's first prayer letter went out in December 1977, an interesting two-page missive which contained not only information about what they had been doing in the year since their marriage, but the challenge that lay before them. God had showed them that their work was to be amongst the visually handicapped, they explained, and then continued, 'A couple was needed who could set up a braille production line which would eventually provide Christian literature and educational text books for India's six million blind. We knew we should volunteer for this task . . . we expect to leave for Madras early in 1978.'

Rona's father had died, but her mother had resettled quite happily in Market Harborough, while of Tony's two sons one was already married, while the other had just got engaged, so they had no anxieties about their families. They put their flat up for sale, stored their furniture, had the necessary injections, packed their bags and set off for India.

* * *

Jeanette Short had long been alerted to the shortage of Christian reading material for blind people in India. Very early in her missionary career she became aware of it, and started to transcribe John's Gospel in Hindi into braille. It had taken her fifteen months, and was produced by Lutheran Braille Workers in the USA. Then Torch Trust in England offered to produce smaller books and booklets, so she continued transcribing and distributing them. Then she found that not only blind Christians, but blind Hindus as well, were eager to have them. This led to a number of the Hindus enquiring about faith in Christ, and Jeanette started to produce a little magazine in braille. The demand for braille Christian literature in Hindi was far exceeding the supply. She had already been seconded by her Mission to work with Christoffel Blindenmission when Tony and Rona arrived in Madras, and was at the airport to meet them. They were to live with her until they were sufficiently accustomed to life in India to find a suitable home of their own, and her help at this stage proved invaluable. She was their only personal friend and advisor in India at the time, and her intimate knowledge of blind people and institutions throughout the country provided Tony with names, addresses, information that would have taken him weeks to collate by his own efforts. She knew the sort of difficulties he was likely to encounter with officialdom, too, and had a piece of good news to pass on as they travelled away from the airport.

'The import clearance licence for the stereotyper and braille press has been granted!' she told them. Normally the granting of such a licence could take as long as eighteen months so, as one of their Indian colleagues said, 'God has worked a miracle!' It was an encouraging start, but things did not always move so quickly, as they were soon to learn. Nearly two months elapsed before they actually received the necessary piece of paper with the import licence number, and then there were shipping delays, and difficulties in getting the machines through customs. Added to that, building on the site for the braille press was so poor it had to be done again, and it was some weeks before electricity was laid on – and even then for lights only . . . . 'We've been here three and a half months, and we're only three months behind schedule', Tony was heard to observe, rather acidly, one day.

'The whole pace of life here is much slower than in the West', wrote Rona, on whom devolved the task of producing the quarterly newsletter that went to the hundreds of friends who they knew would pray for them. 'Appointments almost never happen on time. The obtaining of a radio or driving licence entails much form filling and trekking from one official to another.' Then she added, 'But everyone is most courteous.'

She made comparatively little reference to her own experiences, but for her even more than for Tony the change from Eastbourne to Madras was drastic. It was not only the heat, rising to over 100F, the mosquitoes and the flies, the dust and the musty smells, the crowded streets and the constantly hooting traffic of which they were both aware. She could not see the women in their colourful saris, nor the maimed and pitiful beggars, the bullock carts and the chickens, the goats and the occasional cow wandering at will among the crowds. She was shut in to what she could hear and smell and feel – but she soon knew from experience that she was shut in in another way, a very practical way. She could not go out alone in Madras, as she had in England. Her white cane, which ensured consideration and often actual helpfulness in her own country, meant nothing to the crowds on the streets of Madras. They did not even know what it indicated – that the person carrying it was blind. And even had they known, they would have done nothing about it but to jostle her aside and push her out of the way – perhaps even worse.

Blind? Was she not blind because she had done some great wrong in her previous incarnation? Was she not being punished in this life for what she had done, or failed to do, in the past? It was Karma, the will of the gods . . . Blind? Bah! Get out of my way! . . .

It was not easy being blind in England, but oh, so hard to be blind in India! She had heard about the sufferings of the visually handicapped in Hindu countries, but finding herself sharing this with them, even to what she realized was a very limited extent, deepened her compassion for them. They had no position in the community. There was no place where they could go and be accepted. How did they occupy their time, confined perhaps in a home where they knew themselves to be burdensome, and where they had not been trained for anything?

As far as she was concerned, she knew herself to be loved, she was treated just the same as everyone else in the household, there were things she could do, housekeeping, cooking, helping Tony and Jeanette by typing for them. Yet even so, she was conscious of something lacking in her personal life, here in India. Apart from her Bible, she had nothing to read. She knew of no Indian organization like Torch Trust that could provide her with Christian books and magazines in braille. Tony always responded readily to her plea, 'Please read to me', but what of the many, many blind people who had no-one to whom they could turn? Her own sense of frustration turned her thoughts more and more to them – people who were as visually handicapped as she, but who had nothing and no-one to tell them of Christ. She was glad that the braille press was being installed which would eventually produce Bibles in Indian languages, but how would those Bibles get into the hands of the blind people who so desperately needed the message of life and hope they contained?

Her thoughts turned to the Torch Trust house parties and Fellowships which had obviously met a widespread need among the visually handicapped in England. Something of the same sort was needed in India, but how could it be accomplished?

Those early months in India, when Tony was fully occupied all day, were not easy ones for Rona, who felt there was little that she could do. But she was soon to discover that a wide and effectual door was opening for them both beyond anything they had imagined when they started out.

7

A New Vision for the Blind

The Rev. P.T. Chandapilla, living in Madras, was
rather surprised one evening in 1978 to receive a visit
from an Englishman who introduced himself and his
wife as Tony and Rona Gibb. Chandapilla knew
nothing about them personally, but welcomed them
into his home with typical Indian hospitality when
Tony Gibb explained that they were in India to set
up a braille press, and had close connections with the
Bible and Medical Missionary Fellowship. The reference to BMMF was sufficient for Chandapilla, but he
wondered how his visitors had heard about him?
They had read an article written by him in *Light of
Life* magazine which had deeply impressed them, he
was told, and when they realized that he was a
neighbour they decided to call.

That first meeting was an unusually challenging
one to Chandapilla, and a surprising one, too. Here
was a tall, well-built, middle-aged Englishman, a

typical 'British Raj', in good health and evidently in full possession of his faculties – and he was married to a young Englishwoman, smiling and self-possessed, but whose eyes did not focus, even when her face was turned towards him. It was because she could not see, he realized with a little start of surprise.

Never before had he met such a couple. Only once in all his travels in India (he was an evangelist with a widespread ministry) had he known of a married couple in which one was visually handicapped, and in that case it had been a sighted woman who was married to a blind man. But here before him was an Englishman with a visually handicapped wife. They were obviously happy together, and united in their desire to do something to help blind people in India, his own country. They told him about the setting up of the braille unit and that the aim was to employ 50% of blind people in it. But that was not all. They wanted to help blind people spiritually, socially, emotionally as well as practically. They had been living with Jeanette Short, but now felt sufficiently at home in Madras to rent a flat of their own, and already visually handicapped people were finding their way to it.

'They are so lonely, these visually handicapped people, feel themselves so unwanted', Rona said, adding that so few of them had ever heard about Christ, yet how much they needed him, these doubly blind people. She and Tony kept open house for them, made them welcome, but they wished they could do more. As strangers in India they did not

know how to set about it. They could not even talk
to them without an interpreter.

Tony and Rona could have had no idea at the time
of the vital importance of that contact with Chandapilla, nor did they know the effect it had on him. As
he admitted years later, 'I knew that I needed to be
involved in something like this, because I was not
doing much about a holistic gospel. I believed in the
holistic message of Christ, but I was doing very little
about it. My ministry was straightforward evangelism. The social, physical and other aspects were not
directly involved. Therefore, the work of the Gibbs
challenged me . . . so for a totally new, overseas
couple whatever help I could give in Christ was not
to be stingy.'

As far as the Gibbs were concerned, the contact
had come about in quite an unpremeditated way, for
they happened to be in Indonesia, not India, when
they read the article which had so impressed them
that they wanted to meet the writer. Their
employers, CBM, had asked them to go there to
investigate a braille production project, and it was
while they were in Djakarta that they came across
the article, and were amazed to see that the writer
lived in the same city in India as they did. It is
doubtful if they even knew that he was the General
Secretary of the Federation of Evangelical Churches
of India when they went to visit him. Their purpose
in going was simply to meet an Indian with whom
they felt sure they would be at one spiritually, and
whose writing had been an inspiration to them. But
that first meeting was followed by several others, and

Chandapilla had become a close friend by the time, several months later, when they received a telephone call from the CBM Indian representative explaining that as their services were no longer required on the braille site, their financial support would terminate in three months' time, and their return fare to England be supplied. Return to England within three months!

'We would not be honest if we didn't admit that the news came as a big shock and disappointment to us', they wrote, in what might be termed an emergency letter to their prayer partners, continuing, 'We are still absolutely convinced of God's call to India, and at this stage find it difficult to understand His ways and purposes in the present situation. However, already the experience has thrown us back even more consciously on the Lord.'

Just at this time they had been introduced to a book entitled *Power in Praise* by Merlin R. Corothers, and as they read it together they felt it contained a message for them. It was easy to praise God when all was going well, but the call now was to exercise their faith in praising him in this bewildering situation. It brought them to a new level of spiritual comprehension as they started to do it, and became conscious of a more settled confidence in God. 'Our heavenly Father is helping us to understand that our present circumstances are known to Him – and more than that. We are in the place and position where He wants us at the moment.'

They decided to go round to see Chandapilla. They had already told him about the work of Torch

Trust for the Blind in England, and their desire to see something similar started in India. But what could they do? They were so often frustrated at not being able to communicate with the blind people who visited them. They could see how Christian Fellowship Centres staffed by Indians who had a real love for blind people (including the beggars and the outcastes) could help them practically as well as spiritually, giving advice on what training and resources were available to them, visiting them in their homes, speaking of Christ in personal conversations. They knew from their own experience how ready many of the people who were cut off from so much that sighted people could enjoy were to respond to the love and compassion of Christ. Oh, that the twice-blind of India could be reached with the Good News! But without Indian co-operation, even leadership, their vision could never materialize it seemed. And now, with the termination of their support from CBM, they did not know how God was leading.

Chandapilla's response was heartening in the extreme. He and his church would give them their moral and prayerful backing at this time of crisis, he assured them. They would not be alone in seeking to know God's plan in all this. Furthermore, he had a suggestion to make. Would they consider associating themselves with the Federation of Evangelical Churches for the purpose of sharing their vision for work among the visually handicapped? If so, he would do what he could to find opportunities for them to speak to leaders of the churches about it.

There were several hundred churches scattered over thirteen states in India in the Federation, so the opportunities could be vast. It was for the Gibbs to decide.

'Should we stay on here and seek to interest Indian Christians in the establishing of Christian Centres? Or should we pack up and come back to England to the flat that has not sold, and on which we are paying monthly mortgage payments?' they asked in their emergency letter to their prayer partners, and continued, 'We are being encouraged and challenged by the Lord in this situation, but we know without a doubt that we cannot "take on India" and go forward in any work for the Lord without your active support through prayer and praise. We should like to know whether you can accept this challenge with us. We will be very glad to hear from any of you regarding anything you feel the Lord would have us know at this time . . . .'

Although Sue Relf in Eastbourne received this letter during the busy Christmas season, she lost no time in duplicating it and sending it off to the five hundred or so friends on the Gibbs' list. The response they received was prompt and encouraging. Air letters were delivered day after day, with assurances of earnest prayer on their behalf, often quoting verses of Scripture felt to be specially applicable to their situation.

The Scriptures always meant a great deal to Tony and Rona, but in this period they were even more precious than usual. Some in particular came with power, as in the case of the one brought by their

Indian landlady who hesitatingly said she had been told by the Lord to tell us to '. . . cast your nets on the other side', Christ's word to the disciples who had fished all night and caught nothing. They did not understand it at the time, but they were soon to do so. Early in January Chandapilla approached them with a more positive request than before. He would suggest that the FECI become responsible for the establishing and maintaining of Fellowship Centres for the Visually Handicapped, and that the Gibbs be asked to help for the next two years. The idea would have to be put before the Executive Council, but there seemed little doubt but that it would be accepted.

Fellowship Centres for the blind, established and staffed by Indians, in which they themselves would simply be invited to help with the experience they already had in this field! Was this the 'casting of the net on the other side'? If so, it would mean remaining in India. They longed for a tangible confirmation that it was the way they should take, and it came very soon. They had been praying that if God intended them to stay on, their flat in Eastbourne should be sold quickly. The day after Chandapilla spoke to them they received a letter from the U.K. They saw it was from their agent. Tearing it open they read the news – at last there was a buyer for their flat. The way ahead was clear, and as they wrote in their March letter,

'The next Scripture to which God clearly drew our attention was Isaiah 43: 18–21. "Remember ye not the former things, neither consider the things of old.

Behold I will do a new thing. . . .This people have I
formed for myself; they shall shew forth my praise."
A definite and timely command to put the past
behind us, encouragement regarding the new thing
He was doing at present, and a promise for the
future concerning the blind people of this land.'

* * *

Life for Tony and Rona was very full now. When at
home there were frequent visits from visually handicapped people, ranging from those who were very
short sighted to those who were totally blind. If
conversation was limited in the absence of an
interpreter, the welcome given was always cordial,
and they had both learned how to ask the question,
'What would you like to drink?' If they did not
always understand the reply, the Indian girl who
worked for them was at hand to provide what was
asked for. When the visitors were those who had
been taught English there were always Christian
books and portions of Scripture in braille for them to
read – and to borrow. In fact, they sometimes
laughingly said that their home was turning into a
braille lending library. A telephone call at 7.30 one
morning proved to be from a blind friend working at
the braille press, asking if he could borrow some of
the books of Rona's Bible. He had been a Roman
Catholic, but now he wanted to study the Bible.
There was Hooriya, too, a Muslim, and Kaushalya, a
Hindu, and others who had been taught braille and
longed for something to read. What an opportunity

for them to discover the gospel through their finger tips! Tony and Rona wished they had more literature in braille in Indian languages – but these were in very short supply. It was a need of which they were to become increasingly aware.

The date fixed for the meeting of the Executive Committee of the FECI* was early in April, but before that the Gibbs had responded to a request from an English missionary couple living some 100 miles away to visit them. They had started a training scheme for handicapped people, including the visually handicapped, and wanted advice as to what crafts would be suitable for blind people. 'Eric and Marge Dearman are initiating an exciting and ambitious programme which will have far reaching effects for the blind of India', reported Rona, 'We hope to keep in touch with the project and visit as time permits.'

After that visit they had travelled 1,400 miles to visit the Discipleship Centre in Delhi. This was a Christian centre run by an Australian, Johnson Samuel, about whose work they had heard, and they welcomed the opportunity to see it first-hand. 'Although not exactly the same as we envisage for Fellowship Centres for the Blind, the Delhi work is the only thing of its kind in India, so far as we have been able to discover. It was good to see Johnson at work, and to meet some of his blind friends. He has

---

* FECI is very similar to the Fellowship of Independent Evangelical Churches in England.

an obvious gift for befriending and contacting people, and we are glad to know there is one place at least in this huge city where blind people can drop in for fellowship and friendship.'

From Delhi they travelled by train to attend the FECI. Executive Council in Madhya Pradesh, a journey which at the last stage involved sitting for ten hours on hard wooden seats – 'but it was worth it to travel with Rev. Chandapilla.' And the outcome of the discussions held was to invite the Gibbs officially to work with the 'Commission on Mission' assisting churches to establish Centres where the visually handicapped could come and find Christians ready to offer them friendship and help.

'All these will be the full responsibility of the Indian churches, and they will not be dependent on the West for finance . . . . There is no limit to the part that such Centres could play in sharing Christ with the "twice-blind", integrating them into the local church, and through that into society.'

The first step would be to inspire the churches with a genuine compassion for a section of the community that hitherto had been almost completely ignored. Tony and Rona were invited to attend a Conference in Pune where they would meet pastors, an all-India Youth Conference in the foothills of the Himalayas, and on the way there to visit the well-known Christian hospital complex in Ludhiana. Here a former fellow student of Rona's at the London Bible College, Daniel Abraham, was in charge of the Christian Fellowship Centre, and eager to have a Fellowship Centre for the Blind as soon as possible. At the same time they were urged to return to Delhi to work with Johnson in contacting pastors . . . . Within three months of deciding to remain in India, Tony and Rona were writing that the opportunities were boundless.

The question of their personal support was settled, too. The CBM reversed its original decision, and undertook to provide them with a monthly living allowance.

8

Towards the First Fellowship Centre

It was a good thing for Tony and Rona that blind people and their escorts could travel by reduced fare on Indian railways, for the living allowance provided by CBM naturally did not cover travelling expenses, and they were to be constantly 'on the move' under the terms of their new assignment. The first arrangement made for them involved a 22-hour journey to Pune, and in the hot climate it was like travelling in an oven. The resourceful Tony soon learned how and where to change trains, hail a coolie, and holding Rona firmly by the hand thread his way through the crowds of Indians in saris, in dhotis, in torn rags or smart western suits, hawkers shouting their wares, whole families sitting or sleeping on piles of baggage. For Rona, shut in to what she could hear or smell or feel, the experience of train travelling in India was different from anything she had known in England, for she realized that she could never do it alone. Even with Tony there were times when she was pushed aside or cursed – though it never happened twice. Tony saw to that – he sometimes found it hard to obey the Scriptural injunction, 'In your anger do not sin'. Those who had unwittingly offended found themselves suddenly confronted by a stern-faced Englishman, whose expression of indignation made them shrink back in alarm. What had they done wrong? After all, it was only a woman, and a blind one at that, who had got in their way . . .!

Intolerance of anyone with a visual handicap seemed to be the universal reaction. Even among the sincere Indian Christians Tony and Rona met there was an unconscious attitude of indifference towards those who were blind. The Government was providing Rehabilitation and Training Centres for sightless people, and one such Centre was very near two of the house groups in Pune where they had been invited to speak. No attempt had been made by any of the members of the house groups to contact or offer help to any of the blind people in the Centre. When Tony and Rona went to visit the place the Manager volunteered the information that fifteen of those undergoing training were Christians (as distinct from being Hindu, or Buddhist, or Sikh, or Muslim). Where did they go to church? They did not go anywhere. What church would have them? No-one wanted blind people.

'There is an immediate opportunity in Pune for the opening of a Fellowship Centre for the Blind, and we long that the Christians there will see and accept the challenge', the Gibbs reported.

From Pune they went into a very rural part of Maharashtra State to meet a small group of pastors, then on to Delhi to meet Johnson Samuel again, who was in urgent need of more helpers in the work he was doing. Tony had the opportunity to speak of this at a Delhi Bible Fellowship service held in the Imperial Hotel, where there was one very heartening contact. 'It was good to meet the one who prepares the Far East Broadcasting Association's weekly radio programme for the blind.' Something was being done for them over the air, anyway! They wondered how many sightless people tuned in eagerly every week to listen to that programme so earnestly and carefully prepared especially for them.

'We arrived home just before Easter', wrote Rona to their prayer partners, 'and to give you an idea of the distances we had travelled, imagine a train journey from London to Berlin, on to Prague, Belgrade, and then back to London, all within two weeks.'

Their next journey was south to the Dohnavur Fellowship, where they met with sympathetic interest in what they were doing. 'How could they help?' the members of the Dohnavur Fellowship wanted to know. As they talked about the ways in which blind people among their own Tamil speaking neighbours were in special need, they realized there was practically nothing in the way of Christian books in braille for them. Perhaps this was something that should be done? If some of the members of the Fellowship learned braille, they could eventually transcribe Tamil Christian literature. They knew the value of Christian literature, for the books written by their founder, Amy Carmichael, had influenced so many. Transcribing into braille would be a long, slow process, but it would be worth it to provide blind people with a little of what the sighted had in abundance – something to read.

From Dohnavur the Gibbs travelled to Ludhiana, where Daniel Abraham had arranged a busy schedule of meetings, then on to the FECI. Youth Leadership Training Camp, a sort of house party for young people, held this time in Mussoorie, in the foothills of the Himalayas. The house party was a comparatively small one, but it provided Tony and Rona with the opportunity to mix with the young people on a personal level as well as to share their vision for work among the blind at meetings. One of the other speakers, having listened to them both, and having observed the social and spiritual contribution Rona, though so visually handicapped, had made to the Camp, said to Tony, 'I believe your main task in India is to educate the churches that they have a responsibility towards the blind,' adding rather quietly, 'I've never realized before that I should be involved.' Others were being similarly affected, proving once again the truth of the old adage that example is better than precept.

It is not difficult to assess to what extent the presence in their midst of a sighted husband obviously devoted to his visually handicapped wife, and the natural, uninhibited way in which she behaved was responsible for the outcome of this Camp. Tony and Rona themselves probably did not fully realize how it had affected the young people. The fact remains that it was here that the idea was conceived to make the next Youth Camp different. It should be for sighted *and* blind young people.

The idea was revolutionary from an Indian point of view. So far as was known, nothing of the sort had ever been held before. But not only were the young people themselves enthusiastic about it, the members of FECI. Committee readily accepted the proposition. It was decided that the very next Camp to be held, in October, should also be in Mussoorie and the medium should be in Hindi, making it open for anyone under thirty in North India – sighted or blind.

Neither Tony nor Rona could speak Hindi, but they were to be present at the Camp to advise or make suggestions as required, and as the time drew nearer, feeling their responsibility, they became rather anxious when they heard that applications were coming in very slowly. 'With less than five weeks to go we have only three prospective campers, two blind and one sighted. We have space for fifty people! As we get jittery about this venture, the first of its kind in India, we can only say "God has provided so far, He will bring the people." ' Experienced people to speak and lead the music had been booked, and a large, unexpected gift from the U.K. was helping to cover expenses, but where were the campers? 'We must pray for the RIGHT ones to come', they continued in their September prayer letter. 'We want this to be a happy time, when blind and sighted youngsters can freely mix together, a time when some will come to Christ and others will be built up and strengthened in their faith. Please pray!'

In the event, there were only thirty people in the Camp, which was a disappointment at first, although half were blind, but as the days passed it became evident that God had answered prayer that the *right* people should be there. Everything went smoothly from first to last. The blind and sighted young people were a most enthusiastic group, joining in everything from Bible studies to boisterous games, five of them put their trust in the Lord Jesus Christ, while others who were already Christians were strengthened and inspired in their faith. Nor was that all. The speakers and leaders present, experiencing the joy of seeing visually handicapped people not only living normal lives, but being unusually open to the gospel message, were insistent that this must not be the last of such house parties, but the first. Within a few weeks arrangements were made for other such house parties for blind and sighted people in Mussoorie, while the Child Evangelism Fellowship Camp in Kerala agreed that blind young people could be included, and enquiries about the running of blind and sighted house parties were coming from the Tamil speaking areas of South India. The outcome of that first Camp for the blind and the sighted was more widespread than Tony and Rona had even dreamed. Something had been started which was to continue down through the years, and was to result

in the salvation of many blind people who might
otherwise never have heard the Good News of
eternal life through faith in Christ Jesus.

Meanwhile, progress had been made towards the
establishing of at least one Fellowship Centre for the
Blind. On September 29 the first one was opened by
the Rev. P.T. Chandapilla in a church in Madras.
Every evening in the week, except Sundays, it was
announced, the Centre would be opened for two
hours for visually handicapped people to come and
chat and meet sighted people who would be glad to
get to know them, and give them advice or help them
if possible. Tony and Rona were delighted that at
last they could tell their blind visitors about it – a
place to go where they would meet people who could
talk to them in their own language, who wouldn't
need an interpreter.

'Is it for people of any religion?' one asked. Yes,
all would be welcome, Hindus, Muslims, anyone,
was the prompt reply.

'Can I get my study books read there', enquired
another, a young student whose poor eyesight made
study very difficult. Again the answer was in the
affirmative.

They did not confine their advertising of the new
Centre to those who came to their home, either. On
the crowded Madras railway station one day Tony
spotted a man sitting with a large embossed book on
his knees, over which his fingers were moving while
he droned out the words he was reading. He had a
wooden bowl before him into which passers-by
occasionally dropped a coin. He was a blind man,

reading braille to get money. Squatting down beside him Tony spoke to him and discovered the man understood a little English, so told him about the Fellowship Centre. 'A place where blind people can go?' The man seemed quite excited at the idea, and Tony went on to tell him where to find it and when it was open. By this time he realized he was in the centre of a crowd of surprised and interested onlookers. Here was someone actually talking to a blind beggar! To throw a coin into the bowl was usual enough, but to squat down beside him and talk to him was unheard of.

There were others to be reached with the news of the Centre, too. A blind brother and sister in their early twenties, although members of a well-to-do family, spent their days cooped up in one room, from which all the furniture had been removed except a bed and a table, 'in case they fall over it'. What joy it could bring them to meet other people on a natural, friendly basis!

Tony and Rona were limited in reaching people on a personal level because of their ignorance of any of the Indian languages. They were becoming very conscious of the need for an Indian fellow-worker, one who could be employed full-time, not only in the organization of Camps and Centres, but also in the rapidly growing literary work. There was already a Bible Correspondence Course in Hindi available for Christians living in isolated situations, and its producers, India Every Home Crusade, had given permission to the Sharp Memorial School for the Blind to transcribe it into braille. Jeanette Short had been responsible for this, and now Miss Chandra Singh, who had been brought up from childhood in Sharp Memorial School, was undertaking to correct lessons as they were sent in to her. Such a course needed to be publicised, and introduced to blind Christians.

Then there was the ever increasing demand for Christian literature in braille, especially Bibles. When the Fellowship Centre in Madras was due to be opened it was without the Bible in braille, even in English, let alone any Indian languages. The Gibbs' prayer letter to the U.K. in September included an urgent plea for any braille Bible portions that could be spared, and the response had been so prompt and adequate that the whole Bible was provided, and some to spare. 'We are able to give parts of the Bible to individuals, when we have what they want.'

The postman arrived almost daily at the Gibbs' home with large parcels marked POST FREE – they were books in braille from England for the blind, for which the International Postal Union made no charge. They were received thankfully, but presented the Gibbs with the never-ending problem of finding empty shelves, cupboards, spaces in the hall and passages, and eventually in the living rooms, in which to store them.

Exactly one year from the time when they had been facing the question whether or not it was God's Will for them to remain in India, they were writing, 'This work has grown far more rapidly than we ever anticipated. It is one thing just to be two people, husband and wife, organizing our own programme, but quite another to find that, unsought for, an organization seems to be emerging. Both we and the FECI Committee are realizing that something must be done to get the work established on an organizational basis. This raises all kind of questions', they wrote as they were preparing for a quick visit across the country to Bombay. 'Whatever is decided is going to take a great deal of time, thought and prayer to implement. We need God's clear guidance.' Then they added, 'We feel unequal to the task.'

The outcome was the creation of a Trust called 'India Fellowship For The Blind', – something they had never envisaged when they decided to remain in India.

9

Travel Experiences in India

'Here's a seat, Rona', said Tony, gently edging her towards a bench on the crowded railway station. She put out her hand to feel it, then sat down, smiling, holding on firmly to the bag she was carrying. 'I'll leave you here with the luggage. Won't be any longer than I can help – must find out which platform the train goes from, and when we can get on it.' He put their bags where she could feel them, ensured that she was comfortable, and hurried away, leaving her alone.

It was a situation to which she was accustomed now, and as she sat there listening to the sounds that had become quite familiar she remembered the first time it had happened, on their arrival by air to India. It had been necessary to change planes at Bombay, and Tony had had to find a seat for her at the airport while he went off to make enquiries. How strange it had been, sitting there all alone on a shiny plastic seat along which she found herself sliding! And surrounded by noises, confused noises, voices speaking or shouting in strange languages (she knew none of them, but discerned differences), and a whirring sound which she later learned came from ceiling fans. Noise! No sound proofing in the concrete building, and she had felt she was being drowned by noises that she could not identify. Then at last, through them all had come one familiar sound – Tony's voice telling her he'd got the information he needed, and they could go and board their plane now.

Well, that was in the past, and she was quite accustomed now to sitting at railway stations or airports, while he went off to make enquiries, or change money, or buy food to eat while they were travelling. She could even understand some of the things by-standers were saying if they spoke Hindi – and occasionally there were those who were conversing in rather broken English, if they did not understand each other's language. There were times when she could have joined in the conversation, but usually she kept silent, conscious that she was an oddity among the throngs of people who could see her, but whom she could not see.

. . . Whom she could not see. But all the time there was the awareness of human presence, the indefinable sixth sense that told her when someone was near, even though silent. But there was not much silence. All around her she could hear the sounds that identified individuals – a child's cry, a gutteral voice, a plaintive murmur, discernible to her quick ear amidst the quick gabble and talk, shouts, clatter, whistles, high-pitched yells.

Smells, too. Whiffs of smoke, spicy food, curry, occasionally the aroma of fresh fruit or vegetables, the scent of incense, the smell of hot perspiring bodies, the mustiness of unswept floors and dirty pavements.

And the heat. How hot it always seemed to be in India! But she had become accustomed to it all by this time, after nearly three years in the country. She could sit quietly waiting for Tony to return, though there were still times when she became almost panic-stricken because he did not come back as promptly as expected. What would happen if he was too late to get on the train in which she was seated, and she was carried off without him? It never happened, but her faith was tested more than once as her silent but almost frantic prayers were answered only at what seemed to be the last minute. It was a relief to settle down together for a train journey that would last for hours.

She had found that there were advantages in all this travelling, tiring as it often proved to be. The greatest advantage was that there was time to think, and to pray. At home in Madras there were always visitors to attend to, lists of shopping to make for someone else to do, meals to plan and often cook, letters to answer on the typewriter after Tony had read them to her, others to write in braille to blind correspondents.

She could do none of these things when travelling. Plans about them had to be stored away in her memory, ready to be brought out at the right time. They were always there without having to be searched for. 'You sighted people are always making lists, then mislaying them', she sometimes teased her friends. 'I have my lists in my head, so I know where they are, where to find them when I need them.' Now, as she settled back in the carriage, heard the whistle, felt the train move, she could relax for a little while before applying her mind to preparation for what lay ahead.

In this case, it was a three-day Workshop for Pastors, the first of its kind to be held. Several house parties for sighted and blind people had been held and were likely to continue entirely under Indian leadership when necessary. Fellowship Centres in some cities had been established, the distribution of braille Bible portions in English was continuing, as was the Bible Correspondence Course. A crowning encouragement, especially from Tony's point of view, had been the appointment of two Indian co-workers, John Wilson, and later, Antony, to run the office. Dealing with all the correspondence and the dispatching of parcels had become a heavy burden, taking all Tony's energy day after day, so that he had returned to the flat entirely exhausted. It was a tremendous relief to be relieved of so much administration. Now, with only a few more weeks to go, they were getting ready to return to England for three or four months. But first there was this Pastors' Workshop, and they were taking it very seriously. That a group of pastors should be willing to give up two or three days to come together solely to learn about work among the blind, showed that they were in earnest. As Tony and Rona sat together in the train their minds were soon occupied with final preparations.

There was no doubt that it was to be Bible-based, and Rona knew that the two books she must have with her were the gospels of Luke and John. The well-known story of the man born blind occupied a whole chapter in John's gospel, and it commenced with the very question so often asked in India. Was this blindness the result of the man's own sin, or that of his parents? So even in those days blindness was seen as a punishment, and the fallacy of re-incarnation was implied – for how could the man have sinned before he was born? The Lord's answer was unequivocal. The blindness was the result of no-one's sin. That idea was ruled right out. There was a purpose in the man's blindness – that glory should be brought to God.

The physical healing, wonderful as it was, was not the end of the story. The receiving of sight did not end the man's problems, nor was it even the most important thing that happened to him. The supreme moment of his life was when he knelt before Jesus, acknowledged him as the Son of Man, and received his spiritual sight.

In Luke's gospel there were three passages in particular that contained a message they could pass on. The first came in the earlier verses of chapter fourteen, where the Lord threw fresh light on the matter of hospitality. 'When you give a dinner or supper to your friends and family, to your relations and rich neighbours, they will invite you back, and you will be repaid', he said in effect, 'and that would be the end of it.' Then he went on to enumerate four types of people who were not in the position to return hospitality, but who should nevertheless be invited. They were the poor, the maimed, the lame – and the blind. Rona knew from personal experience what the hospitality of a home had meant to her, and she knew what it meant to the blind people in Madras who found their way to the house where she and Tony lived. They shared with her the loneliness and hopelessness of their lives, and were so thankful to come again and again to the one home where they were welcomed.

'. . . invite the poor, the crippled, the lame – and the blind', said Jesus, adding the promise 'and you will be blessed. Although they cannot repay you, you will be repaid at the resurrection of the righteous'. The promise of repayment was something that lay in the future, but the blessing is in the present, Rona would be able to assure her listeners. The joy and satisfaction of comforting these ignored and despised blind people and seeing them open their hearts to the love of God in Christ more than compensated for the time given to them. It was blessing indeed!

In the same chapter in Luke was one of the parables that Jesus told – that of the rich man who made a great supper and sent invitations to a number of people who, when the time came, made various excuses and did not come. Then the rich man told his servants to go and bring in others to take their place – again it was the poor, the maimed, the lame – and

the blind. These were the sort of people who would
be overlooked – and the instruction to the servants
was to go and bring them, not merely invite them.
Go where they are, take them by the hand, bring
them.

The same message was emphasized later on, in
chapter eighteen, when Jesus was walking among
excited crowds towards Jericho, and a blind man,
begging by the wayside, cried out to him. Jesus,
hearing the urgency in the voice, stood still. And
Luke, the meticulous historian, records that Jesus,
instead of going to him, commanded that he should
be brought. Others were to bring him to Jesus, not
merely tell him to go to him. This incident in the life
of Jesus brought the lesson to be taught down to
practicality. Someone among the bystanders must do
something, go where the blind man was, take him by
the hand, lead him to Jesus. Some of the sessions in
the Workshop would be devoted to discussions and
explanations as to just how this could be done, in
this day and age, in India.

They had some personal knowledge of the deep,
desperate need of blind people in India, knowledge
that had become a burden which they longed to
share with others. There was the case of Dharam
Das, for instance, who lived as a religious blind
beggar in a Hindu temple. He had come to the first
Camp, and there had received Christ as his Saviour
. . . but when he left the Camp he had nowhere else
to go but to live on in the temple. And there was
Karam Singh. He, too, had attended one of the
Camps and received Christ. But his own family had

then disowned him, and he was living in a hostel run by a fanatical Hindu group during his last year of schooling, and then where would he go?

'Pray that the Church out here will see its responsibility', the Gibbs wrote to their prayer partners.

Perhaps the case that had touched them most deeply was the little girl they had been taken to see in a Tamil Nadu village. She was lying outside the closed door of her home, from which the other inmates had gone off to their various occupations for the day. Tony gave a shocked gasp as he looked at her, scarcely realizing at first that what he saw was a living human being. It looked like a bundle of bones covered with dry skin, clothed in a dirty rag. But there was a little wizened face with sightless eyes that turned towards him as he stooped and picked her up gently.

'Pathetic!' he murmured to Rona. 'Never seen anything like it . . . just left to starve . . .'

'Give her to me', said Rona, and she took the little bundle into her arms. 'Oh, poor little thing!' she exclaimed as she felt the bones through the tight skin. And as she cuddled her, something seemed to awaken with the child, responding to the love she sensed. She clung to Rona, then crawled into Tony's lap as he squatted down beside them, the thin brittle little hands holding on to his arm, stretched out to hold her. When at last they had to move away, carefully disentangling themselves from the little arms stretched out towards them, they were near to tears. Those little outstretched arms . . . .

'One of the hardest things we have ever done was to leave that little one locked outside her empty house because, as usual, the family had gone off for the day and left her to starve.'

Not surprisingly, that was not the end of it. Tony had to do something. He couldn't leave that child like that. Correspondence, packing of parcels, all the business of running the office was pushed back while he made enquiries, learned of a mission school for blind children and got in touch with the Indian lady who had founded it, Mrs. Esther Cornelius. It was arranged that the little girl, to whom they had given the name of Mary, should be taken into the school after a necessary spell in hospital. So started a cordial relationship with Esther Cornelius which was to have far-reaching effects of which they had no inkling at the time.

Throughout that very busy year of 1980, which involved for them a great deal of travelling, Tony and Rona kept track of Mary's progress. She was getting stronger, they learned, but then it was discovered that she was deaf as well as blind, so it meant she would probably have to be moved to Bombay, to go to a Deaf-Blind School there.

'We are very concerned about this, as it will mean another upheaval for her', they wrote. It was not the only reason they had for being concerned. They were hearing very disturbing reports of what was happening in Bombay. Blind people from the Tamil Nadu area, who had been educated in Christian schools, were finding their way to Bombay, seeking employ-

ment. Some had found jobs in factories, some were
selling lottery tickets, but all were reported to be
drifting into idolatry, some leading immoral lives.
Living in the slums, cut off from all Christian
fellowship, they were like sheep without a shepherd.
So what would happen to Mary after she finished
such schooling as was available?

All efforts to get even one Fellowship Centre for
blind people opened in Bombay had failed. Several
meetings with pastors who had seemed to be interested had come to nothing. The only tangible
encouragement had come from the Director of
Operation Mobilisation in the city. He had written
asking for braille Scriptures in Hindi and Marathi, as
well as English, saying that since attending one of the
Camps he had started speaking to blind people as he
met them in the streets, and was amazed at how
many there were.

'Seventy thousand of them, in fact', muttered Tony
as he read the letter. Seventy thousand blind people
in Bombay alone. And as the O.M. Director was
finding, many of them, Hindus, Muslims, Buddhists
alike, were willing to receive Christian literature in
braille. Bombay was a harvest field waiting to be
reaped – but where were the labourers?

It was a constantly recurring theme in their
quarterly letters home, this disappointment that
nothing had materialized in the way of a Fellowship
Centre in Bombay. Another one was the need for an
Indian director for the rapidly growing work of
Fellowship for the Blind as it was now called. 'We
still do not have the Director we so much long for',

they wrote in their last letter before returning to England for a few months' home leave. They wondered, as they travelled towards the Pastors' Workshop, whether it would result, eventually, in such an appointment, but although the Workshop went well enough, there was no evidence of anyone emerging to take full-time leadership of the work.

As the time drew near for their return to England, Rona began to feel rather depressed about the whole situation. They had travelled widely, met many people, talked a lot, held seminars, attended committee meetings, done all they could to put before the churches the desperate need of the millions of visually handicapped people in the country – and what had been the outcome of it all? Reports from the two or three Fellowship Centres that had been established were quite discouraging. Sometimes blind people had arrived and there had been no sighted people present to help them, and on other occasions the sighted volunteers who had given precious time to man the Centres had waited in vain for even one blind person to turn up. There was questioning sometimes as to whether the Centres could continue. The Camps, on the whole, were proving spiritually successful, but the blind people invited to them were supported mainly by money collected by Sue Relf in Eastbourne, not by the Indian churches. Some well meaning friends had suggested to the Gibbs that their time and money could be better spent in establishing a school, or an institution, or a training programme.

Tony, the pragmatist, was fully occupied in practical matters. Not only had arrangements to be made about storing their furniture when they vacated the flat, but the newly acquired premises next door to the Chandapilla home had to be fitted with shelves, cupboards, braille units installed, desks, tables, chairs . . . . All was going very satisfactorily. 'We praise God for the way He has provided for all these things . . . wonderful to have all the braille out of our house . . . it completely filled a lorry, lent to us at no cost', Tony reported triumphantly. But Rona, the visionary with more time for reflection about their long-term aims, was dissatisfied.

'We seem to be getting nowhere', she thought, and one morning, alone, she prayed very urgently about it. Ought they to start some institution and just concentrate on running it, she asked? Very quietly, but powerfully, the answer seemed to come in the form of a question. 'Is that what I have told you to do?'

No, she knew it wasn't. What God had told them to do was to share with his church in India what ought to be done about the visually handicapped. 'But, Lord, that's what we've tried to do – but it hasn't worked. So few people seem to respond to the vision and *do* anything.'

'Their reaction to what you say is not your responsibility', was the reply. If she and Tony had been obedient in sharing the vision, that was all that was required of them. 'What they do then is between them and me.'

She told Tony about this 'conversation' with the Lord, and they agreed that it clarified their own pathway. They had been asked by the FECI to return to India for a further three years after their home leave, so that was what they would do. They would share the vision God had given them for the visually handicapped in India as long as he gave them an open door, and the strength to go through it.

10

Some Who Shared in the Work

'As his part is that goeth down to the battle, so shall his part be that tarrieth by the stuff; they shall part alike.' So reads the Authorized Version of 1 Sam. 30: 24. And although the New International Version renders it somewhat differently – 'the share of the man who stayed with the supplies is to be the same as that of him who went down to the battle. All shall share alike' – the meaning is the same. In times of war those who remained at the base, responsible for guarding supplies, were on a par with those who were warriors in the battle field. Tony and Rona in a very practical way applied what they read in the Bible to their own situation. If they themselves might be termed the warriors in the spiritual warfare to bring deliverance to blind people in India, their friends Martyn and Sue Relf in Eastbourne represented those who 'stayed by the stuff'. Their support in prayer, and in circulating their quarterly letters to the large number of friends on their mailing list, as

well as forwarding financial gifts for the work, made
them invaluable team members. To meet the Relfs as
soon as possible on their return to England was a
priority in the Gibbs' programme. It was heart
warming to be able to give full, first-hand reports of
some of the people and situations they had written
about, and to encourage each other as they recog-
nized evident answers to prayer in so much that had
happened.

But they did not confine themselves to visiting
Eastbourne. They wanted to meet other prayer
partners, as well as spending time with Rona's
mother. When they were halfway through their
home leave they were reporting, 'We have taken 23
meetings, slept in 25 beds, visited 64 homes, and
travelled several thousand miles by car.' Even so,
there were many on their list who could not be fitted
into their busy schedule, which included a visit to
Canada to speak in churches there.

This opening in Canada, like so many others, had
come through their friendship with Chandapilla. He
had arranged to meet a Canadian pastor and the
group with him at the airport, and see them settled
into suitable accommodation for the night, and Tony
had gone with him to help. They had met eventually
(they were strangers to each other), but finding
accommodation in the early hours of the morning
had proved so difficult that at last Tony had said,
'Come back to my place.' So back with him they had
gone. Rona, rising hastily from bed, had welcomed
them with her usual sang froid, settled them all
comfortably, somehow – and so had started a

friendship which resulted in extending concern for India's blind people to churches in Canada. For Tony and Rona it had proved a most encouraging – and enjoyable, opportunity.

However, news reaching them from India of the progress of the work was not without its disappointments. The Hindi Camp in Mussoorie had been a great success in some ways, with four of the sixteen blind people present coming to personal faith in Christ, but the organizers had been puzzled that a party of 14 who had booked earlier simply did not turn up. It comprised about a third of those who had been expected and catered for. One of the Camps in the south had been cancelled altogether, due to lack of funds, and in the other two there were very few blind people.

'We felt a little sad at the small number of blind people who had attended the Camps', Tony and Rona admitted. 'But the Lord reminded us that those Camps *had* been held, even in our absence.' Then they went on to report on the good work Wilson was doing in the office in Madras, although here again there were disappointments, this time in the matter of braille productions in Indian languages.

There had been delays in the brailling of Living Bible children's booklets. When the Telugu transcripts were sent to Hyderabad for proof reading, so many mistakes had been found that the work would have to be done again. In the case of The Acts of the Apostles, transcribed in the USA, when all the proof reading had been done it was discovered that the mistakes had been wrongly listed, so the work was being done again. Instructions for brailling the Marathi books were lost in the post. The Hindi books had been done incorrectly . . . .

'The enemy frustrates the production of God's Word in so many ways', they wrote feelingly. Seventeen people, the majority Muslims or Hindus, were taking the *Guide to Happiness* Correspondence Course in English braille, thus providing an excellent method of evangelism by post. But – 'This Course is needed in the main Indian languages too – we need to find braillists and proof readers in these eighteen languages.' Where were the people who would undertake the tedious and exacting work of transcribing a written language, word for word, letter for letter, into the appropriate combinations of the six dots that make up the braille alphabet?

Increasingly Rona in particular was conscious of the need for Scriptures and Christian reading material in braille, in the Indian languages. Even in the Camps, where the handicap of blindness had been minimized, and things had gone so well, there had been one outstanding lack for those who did not know English. There was nothing for the blind campers to read, nothing in braille in their own particular language. Secular material would have been available, Communist propaganda, Islamic material – but where was the Word of God?

* * *

The Gibbs' home leave ended officially on 25th August 1981, the day their flight was booked back to

India. Their furniture was stored in Madras, and at almost the last minute the news had reached them that the flat they had expected to occupy in Delhi was not available. Where were they to go? Their widespread travelling had given them a broad, if sketchy, knowledge of the country, and in the emergency they both found their thoughts turning to a beautiful area where they already had friends, where rents were much cheaper than in Delhi, where the climate was far less hot and humid, and where Rona could go out walking and shopping without an escort. Mussoorie, in the foothills of the Himalayas. Mussoorie, where the Hindi Camps were held. Mussoorie, where BMMF had its welcoming guest-house, Edgehill, long low bungalows with deep verandas, overlooking magnificent views of a range of steep, wooded hills, beyond which stretched the plains of India.

They both saw the advantages of settling there. The climate and living conditions generally made things easier. Tony would be freer to leave Rona alone when it was necessary for him to pay a quick visit elsewhere. She already knew many of the mountain paths along which she could walk confidently, easily finding her way to the narrow, alley-like market with its stalls and open-fronted little shops. There were many Europeans living in the area, and she was in no way the oddity she was always conscious of being when out in the streets of Madras. So to Mussoorie they went, living for several weeks in Edgehill until they found a large, rather ramshackle bungalow part of which they were able to rent.

Hazelwood, Landour, Mussoorie, U.P. became their new address, the home from which they continued their travels and correspondence, reaching out to many individuals and organizations in India. Their quarterly letters to prayer partners were full of information about other people, mainly blind people, and the progress of the work generally – in fact, so full that Rona had no space to relate a little incident in her own life which nevertheless provided material for one of her articles written for a magazine.

It had to do with a black Labrador dog, which belonged to a family who left it behind when they moved away from Landour. The animal, wandering through the market, for some reason attached himself to Rona, following her home and licking her hand when she stretched it out to stroke him. Sensing that the dog was hungry she cooked something for him – and that settled matters as far as the dog was concerned. It wandered no more. Tony was away at the time, but when he returned he was taken aback to find himself challenged outside his own front door. A black Labrador dog that had been lying quietly before it sprang up snarling at him as he approached, and Tony stepped back in alarm. 'Hi, Rona, what's this?' he called out. Rona was soon at the door, smiling as she spoke reassuringly to the dog, then explained it all to Tony. 'We can keep him, can't we?' she asked – rather unnecessarily Tony observed, looking at the animal which had flopped down comfortably and was now eyeing him without animosity. The dog had evidently come to stay and become one of the family – along with the cat.

In some ways life in Landour was easier than it had been in Madras. On the social side, two large boarding schools in the area meant there was a sizeable ex-patriate community mingling with well-to-do Indian families. Happy faced children climbed up and down the steep paths on their way to and from school, their voices carrying far in the clear air. Indeed, there were many sounds that Rona could identify from all over the hills – men calling to each other at work, a mother calling a child, the sound of hammering under the ledge of a cliff, the singing of birds, the chattering of monkeys in the trees behind the house. It was very different from the noise and honking of horns along the streets of Madras.

But as the months passed, Sue Relf, reading the letters that came to her privately as well as receiving the quarterly one she sent out to all prayer partners, perceived that Tony and Rona were not happy.

They seemed discouraged. For one thing Wilson had resigned. 'We are very disappointed and puzzled that he is leaving the work he was doing so well, and in which he seemed so happy. His going is leaving a big hole in the south . . . . This just high-lights once again our desperate need for an Indian director', they wrote in their first letter after returning to India. Otherwise it was full of information, as usual, about blind people they knew, the progress (or otherwise) of brailling Scriptures into different Indian languages, fresh openings for speaking about the work,

and so on. The letters that followed were the same –
but reading between the lines Sue and Martyn
discerned an increasing anxiety about one matter in
particular.

'As always we have so appreciated your letters and
gifts for the work, and without you this could not
have continued.' Then followed an urgent request.
'Pray that your gifts will be matched from *within
India* – we are desperately concerned at the lack of
financial support here. NOT ONE Indian church
gives regularly, though we do get small gifts from
just a handful of individuals here, and NO church
pays any travel expenses of staff when invited to
speak.' Their own living expenses were met by CBM,
but the work and the employed workers were
dependent on voluntary contributions, and these
were coming almost entirely from outside the
country. They shared their concerns with Chandapilla, and it was at his suggestion that two days
devoted entirely to prayer and waiting on God
should be held in Madras in April. 'We realized that
it was only going to be as we sought God in prayer
that we would find our needs met and the work
would progress in God's way.'

They got to a particularly low ebb in May when
Tony had to admit he had never felt so tired before,
and in a letter to the Relfs he continued '. . . we are
asking the Lord many questions. One particular
burden is finance. In all our experiences at Torch
we never got into financial difficulties, He always
supplied even if it was at the last minute. We are
puzzled. Where have we gone wrong? Have we

wasted money in any way? Is there something You are teaching us, Lord? Why are You holding back the money, Lord, especially when we have been stressing to our Board that You will always supply without fail, Lord?'

It was unlike Tony to write in such a vein, the Relfs thought, and they could visualize him pulling himself together as he continued his letter with the words, 'I think I had better close and get on with sorting out the accounts which have a major problem. We are fine, and enjoying life here, and as a friend said to us – with all the frustrations and problems the Lord must be saving up a special blessing.' What their friend said proved to be right.

The Relfs themselves would probably not have claimed to be partners in the work in the way Tony and Rona often implied, for their own lives were full with family, business and church responsibilities in Eastbourne. But something happened about this time which proved they were more deeply involved than they had realized. They received an annuity.

It was quite a large sum of money, and they might easily have found ways of using it at home, but their minds turned almost immediately to Tony and Rona. Tony and Rona were having a difficult time. As they thought about it and prayed about it, both Martyn and Sue felt increasingly that the money should be spent in going to India to visit the Gibbs, just to encourage them. So they made their plans, booked their flights and duly arrived, with their two children, to be met at the airport in Delhi by the Gibbs and taken on the seven-hour taxi ride up to Mussoorie.

Tony and Rona were in good spirits, for the tide had begun to turn – to what an extent none of them could have realized at the time. The first evidence of it had come after a meeting organized by the Union of Evangelical Students at India. One of the young men present had come to Tony and Rona afterwards and said, 'You ought to meet Prabhu and Nancy Rayan. They live in Bombay, and they're working among blind people, like you are.' That was the first that Tony and Rona had ever heard of an *Indian* couple actually dedicated as they themselves were, to bringing spiritual sight and comfort to that despised and neglected class – the blind people of India. Then, when they returned home that same night they found a pile of letters awaiting them, amongst them one from Esther Cornelius. To their amazement it was about an Indian couple in Bombay, Prabhu and Nancy Rayan, who were working among blind people there, and with whom the Gibbs ought to get in touch. Their name and address was included in the letter, and Esther obviously expected them to do something about it.

The significance of the contents of that letter, coming so soon after hearing about the Rayans, was not lost on Tony and Rona. By the time the Relfs arrived in Mussoorie Tony had already written off to Prabhu, and plans were in hand for a meeting between the two couples, one English and one Indian, into whose hearts God had put his own love and concern, for 'the poor, the crippled, the lame – *and the blind*'. So after two weeks in Hazelwood in Mussoorie – 'the children were completely at home and loved their dog and cat' – the Relfs travelled with Tony and Rona to Bombay. They stayed in the Methodist Guest House there, and coming into the lounge on the evening of their arrival were met by a young Indian couple who rose from their seats to meet them.

* * *

Prabhu and Nancy Rayan had been living and working among blind people in Bombay for a year, in response to a call from God, as Prabhu firmly believed. The call had come primarily through Mrs. Esther Cornelius, who was once referred to in a magazine as a dynamo of a woman, a sort of Mother Teresa among Protestants. She had already started four or five schools for blind children, and was visiting Bombay for the rehabilitation of adult blind in that city. What she had encountered had distressed her deeply, and meeting Prabhu unexpectedly she had poured out to him their desperate plight. Then she said firmly and clearly, 'My job is over now. It's your responsibility.' Then she had gone off like a whirlwind, leaving Prabhu transfixed. It was a revolutionary thought that would not leave him. His responsibility.

Reading in Luke's Gospel he came to the words in chapter four, verse 18. 'The Spirit of the Lord is upon me because he hath anointed me to preach the gospel to the poor; he hath sent me to heal the broken hearted, to preach deliverance to the captives, and recovering of sight to the blind, to set at liberty those that are bruised.' He had read them many times before, but now they spoke directly, confirming, as it were, God's call to him through Esther Cornelius. Finally, in church one day, his attention was drawn to the words the choir was singing,

> Consecrate me now to Thy service, Lord
> By the power of grace divine,
> Let my soul look up with a steadfast hope
> And my will be lost in Thine.

He saw it was written '*by Fanny Crosby, a blind lady*'. There could be no doubt now – the Rayans were called to work for and among blind people. It was 1981, the International Year of the Disabled, and the Indian Government was doing a lot in practical ways to improve life for disabled people, including those who were visually handicapped. But what about their spiritual needs?

The Rayans' home became a centre to which blind people could find their way any and every day, and where they were introduced to the Word of God and to Jesus, the Saviour of mankind. But as time went on it was impressed on Prabhu that the task of reaching blind people was too great for them alone. They tried to encourage new believers to go to church locally, but somehow it did not work. If they went at all, they soon stopped going – no-one took any notice of them.

'Nancy', said Prabhu one day. 'I think we must have a meeting of all pastors and lay readers and put before them the need of evangelising the visually handicapped people, and integrating them into their churches.'

'But how can we do it? We have no expertise. We wouldn't know how to set about it.' Prabhu was more confident. If the Lord was guiding them, he would send the right people to help them.

As they were talking the door bell rang, and the postman handed over an envelope. Prabhu looked at it, saw it was from a stranger, and ripped it open. This is what he read,

'Dear Prabhu and Nancy, We heard about you and your involvement with the visually handicapped people through Mr. Errol Kantharia and also through Mrs. Esther Cornelius. Since we are in Bombay during the second week of August, could we meet you . . .?' The letter was signed 'Tony and Rona Gibb'.

So that is how it came about that on 14th August, 1982, the two couples met for the first time, the Relfs standing back, silent onlookers. 'Tony!' Prabhu called out, and Tony turned towards him. 'Prabhu!' he exclaimed excitedly, stretching out his hand. Then he introduced Rona. 'This is Rona, my wife', he said, adding quietly, 'She is blind.'

Any natural barriers that existed between East and West were broken at that moment, and almost before they realized what was happening they were embracing each other as though they were old friends.

It was the beginning of an association that had all the evidences of being divinely planned, and the final confirmation, as far as the Rayans were concerned, came the following evening. Prabhu still had a reservation in his mind regarding co-operating with Westerners. He wanted to be involved in a work that was entirely indigenous, in no way dependent on Western influence – or money. He said as much to Nancy.

'If the Gibbs talk about money, we won't have anything to do with them.' He was very definite about it. They were preparing for the first anniversary of the meetings they had been holding each week in their home, and had invited the Gibbs and the Relfs to attend. There were about forty people crowded together in the small room, many of them blind. All of them sat on the floor, and as the meeting was conducted in Tamil the two English couples naturally did not understand much, though they all agreed it was a highlight for them. Towards the end of the meeting Prabhu realized he had not given Tony an opportunity to say anything, so looked across at him and said, 'Brother, will you please speak something from the Bible?'

Tony, quite unprepared, with a quick prayer in his heart, stood up, turned to Acts chapter three, spoke for a few minutes and then concluded with words which caused Prabhu and Nancy to glance quickly at each other, an amazed but joyful glance, which no-one but themselves would have understood. 'I don't have silver and gold, but I can offer you what I have – Jesus Christ and his love.' No talk about money there – rather a repudiation of it! The Rayans had no doubt after that – God intended them to work with the Gibbs.

It was an historic occasion, of vital importance to the work among the blind in India, though none of those involved could have realized it at the time. A few days later the Relfs boarded the plane that took them back to England, to take up the threads of their life there. But they returned with a new vision. They had seen with their own eyes what had been conveyed only through what they had read before. The memory of those blind people gathered in the Rayans' home, poor people, some of them dressed in rags, with their faces looking up sightlessly as they listened to what was being preached and read was to remain with them, an incentive to play their part in the spiritual warfare – to 'tarry by the stuff'.

11

Trusting God in All Situations

'We must give the camel room', said Chandapilla.
'room to have its own quarters.' If the observation
raised a smile on the faces of those sitting around the
table, the inference was obvious. The occasion was a
meeting of the Executive Committee of the Federation of Evangelical Churches of India, and the matter
under discussion was its relationship to the 'India
Fellowship for the Blind'.

The moral support and backing of the FECI had
been of inestimable value, when it had readily
accepted the untried Fellowship as an auxiliary.
Tony and Rona could never forget it. However, with
the rapid and unpremeditated expansion of the
work, especially since the association with Prabhu
and Nancy, being an auxiliary to any one group of
churches could prove more of a hindrance than a
help. 'So it was decided that the "camel" should be
allowed to have its own quarters', wrote Rona in the

first quarterly letter in 1983. 'This is in no way a break, we look forward to uninterrupted fellowship as an associate member, but it is going to free us to take staff and Board Members who are not themselves involved with FECI . . . . During the next six months we have to complete the necessary registration and legal formalities.'

They were very grateful to leave the legal formalities, which proved more complicated than they would have expected, to Rev. Panallal, President at FECI. Among other things, the name of the Trust was changed, highlighting again the particular stigma in India attaching to the very word 'blind'. Although they had been conscious from their earliest days in the country of the peculiar difficulties which sightless people encountered, after five years they had come to realize that the very word was almost like a curse. Even Nancy Rayan had a story to tell against herself of the days before her heart had been touched with compassion for the sightless. She had been in the first class compartment of an electric train when the giggling of a little group of schoolgirls attracted her attention. Looking up she had seen a man with his eyelids sticking together in the hollow eye sockets, groping his way forward helplessly, stick in hand. His clothes were dirty and ragged, and suddenly there was a chorus of indignation from the other occupants of the compartment.

'A blind man!'

'The audacity – getting into a first class compartment!'

'A ladies' compartment, too', piped in one of the schoolgirls.

Then came the words, 'Let's teach him a lesson!' And as the train came to a halt at the next station the door was flung open and the sightless man pushed ruthlessly out onto the platform.

Nancy had sat quietly in her seat, taking no part in what the others were doing, but she admitted that she had thought to herself, 'He deserves it! Blind people are no better than beggars – a liability in society.' She told the story freely, to demonstrate the almost universal attitude towards sightless people. So what was the best way to describe them without using the word 'blind'? After all, even blindness was comparative, as Rona herself knew. She could distinguish the difference between light and darkness, discern very vaguely the outlines of buildings, porches, stationary vans. Others could see nothing whatever before them, but had a little sight at the side of one eye. And so on. Otherwise they were just like everyone else – could hear, smell, feel, taste, use their hands, walk and talk, think. Their only handicap was visual. They were visually handicapped. So the Trust was given a new name. 'India Fellowship for the Visually Handicapped'.

Interestingly enough a year or two later it was decided to set up a similar sort of Trust in England. Sue Relf had been forwarding money to India sent by individuals for the work the Gibbs were doing. Someone pointed out that it would be simpler, and save money, if it were done through a charity and a

Trust was formed called 'Fellowship for the Visually Handicapped'.

In the Deeds the Solicitor rather surprisingly included a clause to the effect that the Trust could produce Christian literature in braille for India and other third world countries. There were some who demurred at this being even mentioned, and no-one really wanted it, but eventually, with a shrug of the shoulders, it was agreed no harm could come of its inclusion. It was typical of solicitors – they thought of the most unlikely contingencies.

Not all went smoothly in the process of reconstruction of India Fellowship for the Visually Handicapped (IFVH). In September 1984 the Board met while Tony and Rona were on home leave for three or four months, and when they received the Minutes of the meeting they were almost overwhelmed with dismay.

First of all they learned that Prabhu, who had been appointed Promotion and Training Officer, had resigned the post. He had been given the choice of going to work in Maharashtra, where he did not know the local language, or becoming a Trustee, in which case he would receive no salary.

'Prabhu is a man of faith and has proved that God does supply his need. He has chosen to be a Trustee, but has no specific area of responsibility now . . . all field work seems to have come to a halt.'

Secondly, it had been decided that no Camps should be undertaken unless many months ahead there was sufficient money in hand to pay for them.

Funds were low at the time of the Board meeting, so no Camps were planned.

'And it is through the Camps that so many come to Christ!'

'The IFVH Trust Deed states clearly that it is a Faith Fellowship, and we feel absolutely convinced that it is as such that it should continue', wrote the Gibbs feelingly. 'In the five years that the work has been in existence, when we have been sure that a Camp or other means of outreach is the Lord's Will, we have gone forward in faith, trusting God to supply. He has always done so, sometimes at the last minute, and only once have we had to delay payment.' The Camps were so important.

Thirdly, Nancy Rayan, in charge of the braille production programme was being restricted in her contacts with the Bible Society. And lastly, what hurt Tony and Rona personally, was the decision that they should not communicate with any member of staff except through the honorary Director, a blind factory worker in Delhi.

It was a very traumatic period for the Gibbs, intensified by changes and upheavals in the political realm. For the first time they were required to obtain visas before they could return to live in India. Coming events were already casting shadows, although they had no inkling yet of what the future held for them. Others who had previously entered and lived in India without difficulty were having the same restriction – a visa was now necessary, although in most cases it was granted without too much delay or difficulty.

What was far more alarming was the assassination of Mrs. Gandhi, throwing the whole country into chaos. The horrifying scenes of violence that followed the assassination did not leave peaceful Mussoorie unaffected – several shops in the market were looted and furnishings and stock destroyed. This occurred less than a week after Tony and Rona returned to Hazelwood, and arrangements they had made to visit Calcutta, Madras and Bangalore had to be cancelled due to curfews and disruption on the railways.

What was in their minds more than anything else was what should be their relationship with IFVH now. They had accepted the position of consultants only, believing that the Fellowship should be entirely indigenous, but what were they to do now that events had taken so strange and disturbing a turn? After much prayer and discussion they decided to write and explain to the Board that they no longer felt free to act as consultants, but to ask for a meeting with the Trustees. Having done this and posted the letter they waited – and waited – and waited.

'It's at times like this that the problems of communication are high-lighted', they wrote. 'There's no such thing as picking up the telephone to sort things out directly. We are at the mercy of the slow postal service.'

There was only one really encouraging matter to report in that, their first letter to their prayer partners after returning to India. It had to do with a Prof. Don Rogers, a computer expert who was going

ahead with the preparation of a computer programme for the production of braille Scriptures in
the Hindu language. He was being helped by Jeanette
Short, whose specialized experience in braille in
Hindi was invaluable.

'The possibility of using a computer for this work
is tremendously exciting', wrote Rona. If the production of Bibles in braille could be speeded up what it
would mean to the many, many sightless people of
India who had no portion of God's Word they could
read for themselves! Rona often thought of the
young man who had made a special journey from his
home to ask them for a braille New Testament in
Telugu for his visually handicapped sister. Telugu?
Sadly they had had to tell him there was nothing in
braille in that language. Rona had thought often of
him returning empty-handed to a girl whose hopes
were to be so grievously disappointed. Not one
portion of the Word of God that she could call her
own, read for herself . . . .

What Don Rogers was attempting now could
mean so much for India. In the International Year of
the Disabled an order had come through from Russia
to the United Bible Societies in Stuttgart for 500
braille Bibles, and it had been Don Rogers who had
written the programme. Could what he had done in
Russian be done also in the languages of India?

The thought of it was the one bright spot on an
otherwise dark scene. They had sufficient confidence
in their prayer partners to whom their quarterly
letters went, to write frankly, and they did not

disguise the fact that they had been having a bad time.

'Some days we feel discouraged that at a time when blind people are hungry to hear the good news of Christ, and when we had the personnel and facilities to go ahead and expand, the work should be brought to a virtual stand-still. It reminds us that Satan will use any means to stop God's work, especially when he sees it is fruitful.' But it had not stopped there, and their very inactivity practically had proved to be of spiritual benefit, for they had used their time profitably. 'During these weeks we have been able to draw near to our Lord in prayer, and He has drawn very close to us, assuring us that He is in control of what appears to be such a muddle. He has assured us that He brought us back to India, and that the "New Thing" which He promised to do will be accomplished. Nothing can stand in the way of His work, set-backs are only temporary, and are experiences which He can turn to our good. The assurance of your prayers has been a great source of strength.'

The long awaited reply to the Trustees requesting a meeting was eventually received, and after further delays and re-arrangements a date in March was agreed on. It was to be preceded by a short Prayer Retreat – Tony and Rona felt this was essential, and it certainly paved the way for what could have been a rather acrimonious and indecisive gathering. As it was, the study of the life of Abraham, the man whose faith finally triumphed after several lapses, provided an apt prelude to the subject under discussion. This was primarily whether or not the India Fellowship for the Visually Handicapped was to be an organization governed by worldly principles or a fellowship based on faith. The majority of those present were convinced that God was calling to a fellowship of faith.

One outcome of the meeting was that three of the Trustees felt they should resign, but:-

'We want to stress that their resignation is not a break, and that God has helped us all so that we still remain a fellowship', wrote Tony and Rona. 'In the light of Christ's words in Matthew 5: 23–24, we are reconciled, and all of us have experienced God's healing and forgiveness where we hurt each other.'

The Trustees who remained, including Esther Cornelius and Chandra Singh were all of one heart and mind, and things went very smoothly after that. Pastor Joseph was elected as Chairman, Nancy Rayan was invited to be Secretary, and to crown it all Prabhu Rayan was asked to become Director of IFVH

At last there was found an Indian director of the work – something for which the Gibbs had longed and prayed for years. And that he should be such an one, a man after their own heart, whom they already knew and loved, was almost more than they could take in. '. . . we are thrilled. We feel certain that those truly called by God are in the right positions within the Fellowship', was how they expressed it, but the words were really inadequate to convey the deep sense of satisfaction and thankfulness with which they returned to Hazelwood. Their visas were nearly due for an extension, and they decided to ask for the longest period granted – one year. They did not anticipate any difficulty, although they knew there were some ex-patriates who were having to leave the country at short notice, while others were unable to re-enter, except as tourists. A new era had started as far as missionary work in India was concerned.

The date for the next Trustee meeting was fixed for September, and there was a lot to be done before that. The Camps were to be re-started – a Hindi Camp in Mussoorie in May, to be followed immediately by a Tamil Camp in the southern tip of India, and probably a Bengali Camp in October. Links with the Bible Society of India were being strengthened – the work of producing and distributing braille was new to that organization, and Tony and Rona were given two hours in Bangalore to explain about it to auxiliary secretaries from all over India. It was a strategic opportunity to give widespread publicity to the use of braille, and the Bible Society's responsibility in this field.

In early September a workshop had been arranged, and this proved to be a particularly encouraging time. Thirty-four people attended, including a number of pastors. They were together for three days, demonstrating, discussing and personally experiencing some of the problems of the visually handicapped by going around blind-folded at times. Some of the participants came from quite distant areas, which involved sacrificing a week's work, and gave evidence of determination to go back and 'do something'.

It was immediately after this that the next Trustee meeting was planned, and it was with eager anticipation that the group gathered. The agenda was well prepared, and as it was gone through, item by item, there was a spirit of cheerfulness and harmony throughout. Sometimes there were differences of opinion, but when this happened it seemed almost instinctive to stop talking and pray – and very soon the matter was solved to everyone's satisfaction. Tony and Rona could not exchange glances, but an occasional quick grip of the hand conveyed from one to the other the deep consciousness both felt that India Fellowship for the Visually Handicapped was in the right hands. It was truly indigenous.

The meeting was drawing to a close. The only item left on the agenda was to decide the date of the next meeting, and diaries were being consulted when there was a knock at the front door. Tony jumped up to answer it, and after a couple of minutes returned with an expression of dismay on his face and a slip of paper in his hand. It was from the District Superintendent of Police, instructing him to report at the Foreigners Registration Office on the following morning. It came as a shock to all, for they knew it could mean only one thing. It had to do with the extension of the Gibbs' visa, and the wording of the order left little hope that the extension would be granted. There was only one thing they could do.

'Let us pray', said Pastor Joseph, and as they did so there crept into their supplications a note of praise at the timing of the order. It had arrived just as the business had all been got through, and if God had ordered it so, would he not continue to guide?

*   *   *

The next morning Tony reported to the District Superintendent of Police and was served with a notice which read:-

To Mr. Anthony Douglas

Gibb

British National.   P.P.No. N255931 B.

You entered India on 26.10.84 via Delhi Airport. I am directed to inform you that your further extension to stay in India beyond 25.9.85 is rejected by Govt. of India. You should wind up your affairs and arrange to leave India within two (2) months from the date of issue of this notice. If you fail to comply to this order you shall be liable to be prosecuted . . . .

12

Return to England

'Wind up your affairs and arrange to leave India within two months.' This was the ultimatum, and Rona was conscious of the heavy breathing of those with her as they sat silently, absorbing what it would mean to them personally as well as collectively.

She knew instinctively what Tony was thinking. That practical mind of his would already be grappling with all that winding up their affairs involved: the sorting of possessions, deciding what was to be kept and what disposed of. There would be packing, storing, dispatching, writing to Banks and Insurance offices. People would have to be notified. Appointments beyond the departure date would have to be cancelled. She couldn't do much to help him beyond telling him where things were, remembering names and addresses, reminding him when matters were urgently needing attention, collecting items needing to be packed, but she would do all she could.

She could only guess what the news meant to Prabhu and Nancy, but she realized that it must be almost alarming. The character of their three bed-roomed bungalow had already been drastically changed when Prabhu became leader of IFVH and had set up an office in his own home, since there was no other accommodation available. Two thousand boxes of braille had been mailed from the office in Madras, and Rona and Tony had spent ten hectic days helping to fit them in. They knew from personal experience what it was to have piles of braille books in the corridors, in the bathroom, in the bedrooms and in the kitchen. Nancy had admitted to Rona that she hadn't realized what would be involved until they actually started setting up the national office in the lounge, leaving only a very small space as a living room. With their little girl to consider as well, it had not been easy. Now that Tony and Rona had to leave, a lot of the office equipment they had in Hazelwood must be added.

As for Prabhu, he had taken over the leadership with the knowledge that the Gibbs were still deeply involved as consultants, and could be relied on to continue to run camps and seminars. They were, indeed, the mainstay for that branch of the work. But now, what would happen? Would they always be able to come back on a tourist visa, when camps were arranged? Tony was the one with whom he could share difficulties, could work so closely with, that to lose him would be like suddenly losing a partner. Was that how Prabhu was feeling?

But most of all Rona was conscious of what it would mean to her. More than any of the others, Indian or western, she was knit in heart to the people for whom they were working – the sightless people of India – ten million of them. She knew, as none of the others sitting with her now could know, the emotional as well as the physical strain, of being blind. It had meant so much to her to receive some of them into her home, welcome them, make them realize they were understood and appreciated as normal human beings. In the frequent long and tedious journeys she and Tony had made it had always been with the satisfaction of knowing they were doing it to alleviate the sufferings of the people on whom the very appellation of the word 'blind' was like a curse. And more than that, over and above all was the urgent desire to reach them with the news of God's love for them. The joy of sensing, as had so often happened, the change in them when they had experienced for themselves that love! She had detected the change, even in their voices. Now that was all to end, as far as she was concerned. Hazelwood in Mussoorie would soon not be home any more. In fact, they would have no home. They did not even know where they would go. It was one thing to be ordered out of India, but to where? Tony had received requests to go to Pakistan and Nepal.

The question now was to discover what the Lord's plan was for them. In the midst of all the perplexity and disappointment faith reassured her that God had a purpose in it all.

The presence of Pastor Joseph and the Rayans at this time was of inestimable comfort. 'It is impossible to describe what their loving friendship and support has meant.' They remained on for two days after the ultimatum had been received, and it was as Pastor Joseph was leading them in a devotional session on their last morning together that Tony and Rona received the answer to their very urgent prayer earlier. 'This morning we asked God to show us specifically from His Word whether we should make plans to return to England, or go immediately to some other country', they wrote. 'The passage to which God had directed Pastor was from Luke 8. We discussed various verses, and then Luke 8. v. 39 jumped out at us. "Go to your house and tell the great things God has done for you." '

They were in no doubt after this but that they should return to England. Looking at their situation objectively they realized that most of what they had been doing recently, particularly the braille work in connection with the Bible Society, could be done from anywhere in the world. Having a clear sense of direction was reassuring, and there were times when they even felt a thrill of excitement in wondering what lay ahead for them. They were sure it still had to do with the India Fellowship for the Visually Handicapped. All the same, it was one of the saddest periods in their lives, and although Rona's quarterly letters, as always, were full of information and encouraging reports of what was going on in India among the visually handicapped, little glimpses of what they themselves were feeling stole through.

'We dread the packing, the thought of leaving our many friends and the lovely place where we have lived so happily . . . .'

'We had no time to think of anything except getting out of India in the time given us. Our Mussoorie friends helped in so many ways, and saying "goodbye" to those who shared so closely with us was not easy. Several of them are also facing the prospect of packing up and leaving because their visas have not been renewed.'

'It seems strange to be thinking of celebrating Christmas in England after spending the previous seven in India.'

Perhaps the most poignant experience of all was when Prabhu and Nancy and little Neena came to stay with them for the last time. They had come, not only to say goodbye, but for the practical purpose of conveying all Tony's office equipment back to their own home. When Tony and Rona stood on the platform of Dehra Dun station, waving as the Bombay train drew out carrying the Rayan family, plus desk, filing cabinet and trunks full of office files and equipment, their emotions were too strong for any conversation. Tony just gripped Rona's hand and led her gently back – back to the house that now seemed so empty and purposeless, a home no longer. A short time later they themselves left it for good, to return to England.

* * *

'Go back to your house and tell what great things God has done for you.' The word that had come to them so clearly on the memorable occasion two months previously, when with Pastor Joseph they had meditated on Luke 8, was the only clear directive they felt they had been given. Home was England, so to England they had come, but writing to their prayer partners less than a week after arriving they admitted they felt bemused at the prospect of settling down there. India was still in their minds and hearts, and as they moved into the bungalow in Hove lent to them by a friend it seemed like entering a void. Suddenly, from a life so full that their diaries had bookings for months ahead they found themselves with nothing to do except keep up with family and friends, and decide where to live.

Only one thing was certain. 'Wherever we live our link and commitment to the work in India will continue', they asserted. And in order to ensure this was done, they went on to explain, 'The Trust (Fellowship for the Visually Handicapped) is now registered and Sue Relf will hold the bank account as before. We want to continue to bless the visually handicapped in India in a financial way, even though we are now in the U.K. ourselves. Any gifts will be forwarded as before.' This matter having been made clear, they set about looking for a house that could become their home. Devonshire was the county they thought they would like to live in, so motoring down to that south-west area of England they came to a small, picturesque town on the edge of Dartmoor. Here in Moretonhampstead they had stayed on a previous holiday, and had been rather charmed with the place, with its narrow streets and front doors opening onto the pavements, its little cobbled alleys leading unexpectedly to courtyards and cottages.

And here, on the outskirts of the town on the Exeter Road, Tony spotted a house for sale. It was in a very old fashioned condition, but that did not deter him, and once again Rona's visual handicap proved almost an asset as she might have protested that it needed to much work to modernize it. As it was, Tony pointed out the ideal position of the kitchen, how it could be elongated to contain a dining table right by the big bay window overlooking the terraced garden and the moors beyond, that there were two rooms that could be turned into a most convenient large lounge, and bedrooms upstairs that could soon be decorated – and Rona was satisfied. Less than two months after leaving India they were notifying their prayer partners that their permanent address in Devon was Sunnymead, Exeter Road, Moreton-hampstead.

Within three months they had joined the local Baptist Church and were getting to know fellow believers in other denominations whom they met at prayer meetings; were arranging to travel to East-bourne and other places to speak at meetings and meet many of their friends who had been supporting the work among the visually handicapped in India; and almost unconsciously were obeying the instruction, '. . . and show what great things the Lord has done for you'. It was instinctive to talk about India, about the blind people there, about those who had been reached with the gospel, about what was going on in the Fellowship Centres, the Camps, the Workshops. What else was there to talk about, anyway? These were the matters that were in their hearts, and there was so much to tell, especially about the individuals they had known personally, and whose progress they still followed.

For instance, there was Ram Prasad, whom Rona had first contacted by responding to his request for a pen pal in a secular braille magazine. He had come to Christ at one of the Camps, and was now preparing for the Christian ministry . . . .

There was Mary, the pathetic little bundle of skin and bones, now an intelligent young teenager, doing so well at school that there was the likelihood of her being sent to USA to complete her education. There was Hooriya, a blind lady in a Muslim home who Rona had kept in touch with from the time a letter had been received from her at Torch Trust for the Blind, asking for braille Christian literature. Visits to her in her Muslim home were always welcome – was she a secret believer?

Then there were IFVH staff workers, like Sankpal who had first been contacted through a Bible correspondence course, and Paran, led to the Lord by Prabhu. He had bowed to family pressure and married a Hindu girl, but she had come to the Lord, and he was now the IFVH staff worker in Bombay. And so on.

But there was one matter about which they had little encouraging news to pass on. In spite of repeated efforts to get the Scriptures produced in braille in Indian languages, all seemed to have proved abortive. With a steady stream of blind people coming to faith in Christ from the different language groups, the need to provide them with the Word of God in their own languages was becoming urgent. Time and time again a start had been made, and come to nothing. It was a slow process at best, for it required readers who could read to blind people in the different languages for them to transcribe into braille, then the material had to be proof read, and several times the corrections were so many it all had to be done again.

Writing in 1986 Rona reported,

'BRAILLE. A main cause for concern at the moment is the production and distribution of braille Christian literature in the Indian languages. Production seems to have come to a virtual standstill, and we need to pray urgently against the many frustrations that the enemy brings. We understand from India that the Madras Braille Press has had to close down, and we do not know whether outstanding orders for Tamil, Hindi, and Malayalam placed by the Bible Society have been fulfilled. It does mean that we shall have to look elsewhere for future productions of braille Christian literature . . . .'

* * *

To look elsewhere for future productions of braille Christian literature.

The sentence appeared in the middle of a two-page letter containing, as usual, information about different aspects of the work in India. For the next three years those letters were written quarterly, with little or nothing to indicate that prayer about this particular matter was being answered. There were occasional references to Professor Don Rogers, the computer expert, who was working on a programme of braille in Hindi, but that was all. During this time Tony and Rona visited India twice, taking part in camps and seminars, travelling thousands of miles in the country by train, bus and occasionally by plane. It was on the second trip that the outstanding need was re-emphasized. Everything else seemed to be going well. More and more blind people were being reached, fellowship centres established, camps held in new areas, churches extending warm welcomes to Christians who were sightless. But what worried Rona most at a meeting of the leaders of the work was the repeated reference to the lack of Bibles in braille.

'I have 1,500 people wanting to read the Bible', said the man from Gujarat State. 'I can distribute 1,500 of any Gospel you can send me within a month of receiving them and I could tell you exactly where each copy has gone to. My Gujarathi blind friends are crying out for God's Word in their own language.'

'I don't have 1,500 people wanting to read the Bible', said the man from Maharashtra State, 'but there are 500 I can pass books on to immediately. They have only one Gospel in Marathi, their mother tongue.'

'Our work is definitely hindered because we do not have the whole Bible in the Tamil language', chimed in another. 'We only have part of the New Testament . . . .'

Then the office manager jumped to his feet. 'We get letters every week asking for braille Scriptures in the Indian languages', he announced. 'We have about 400 people who can read English but there are many, many more who can read braille in their own language, but who don't know English. They want the Bible to read in their own language.'

The question they all put to the Gibbs, rather helplessly, was 'What are you going to do about it?' That challenge was still in the Gibbs' minds four months later when they visited professor Don Rogers and his wife Lilian to discuss the whole matter of braille production in Indian languages. Don had been working laboriously with Jeanette Short, on a Hindi computer program based on romanized scripts, but now on a visit to Wycliffe Bible Translators at Horsley Green he had been given the name and address of a man who had a new computer programme in the Devanagari script (used by Hindi, Marathi and Nepali languages), and this would be better and would ensure accuracy. From him Don was given a copy free of charge so that he could work on it and see if it was versatile enough to produce a braille programme.

In less than three weeks he had the basis of a programme to convert the Hindi script directly into braille. Then he explored the possibility of doing the same thing in other Indian languages. By the time Tony and Rona visited him in December, 1988 he was able to tell them, 'My computer program to produce Hindi braille is ready to run.' He paused a moment, then said impressively, 'And it could be produced not only in Hindi. I could eventually produce it in all Indian languages.'

It was staggering news. Suddenly a whole vista of opportunity opened up. It was as though they had been climbing up a steep pathway through a steamy tropical forest to arrive at the top of a range and see before them a vast, open countryside with roads stretching in all directions, away to the horizon. The possibility of braille Bibles in all the Indian languages. Blind people in all parts of India with the Word of God at their finger tips.

Then came the sobering thought – who would produce these Bibles? As they all knew, braille presses around the world were running at full capacity. Modern computer technology had revolutionized production, and there was more work waiting to be done than could be dealt with. The production of portions of the Bible in at least fourteen major Indian languages was a colossal task, and they knew of no organization that would take it on. A new one would need to be started, and who was to do it?

The professor, in his eagerness to provide those blind believers in India with what they longed for, suggested that he himself might become involved in the actual process of the braille production. Set up a unit right there where they were living, in Bexhill . . . . At this point his wife broke in. 'I am definitely not in favour of it', she said firmly. 'Don already has too much to do. He's often working on his computers into the early hours of the morning. He simply has not the time to set up a braille press. And it's not his line, anyway.' Then she added something which Rona later described as being followed by a stunned silence. *'I think that should be Tony's work'*

13

Compass Braille is Set Up

It did not take long for Tony to make a reply to that challenging remark, 'I think that is Tony's work.' The full implication of what would be involved in setting up a braille unit and producing Christian literature in Indian languages dawned on him almost immediately. First of all, the Braillo itself would cost about £60,000. Added to that would be needed paper, a paper punch, a cutter, cover boards, binding, boxes, not to mention office equipment such as desks, tables, chairs, and also stationery. All told, it would cost about £90,000.

£90,000! Where would that come from? There had been times when the cost of a camp in India, amounting to £400, had seemed to come in very slowly. £90,000! And that wouldn't be the end of it – just the beginning. There would be the continuous outlay on paper and equipment, like computers, not to mention employment of staff.

The short, pregnant silence was broken when Tony said almost in alarm, 'I don't want to!' Then he added, rather lamely, 'It needs someone younger.' After all, he was already in his sixties. It was too late in life to start an entirely new type of business. He was more than willing to motivate someone else to do it, would give all his experience and expertise freely, put his administrative ability at the disposal of whoever took on the responsibility of running a braille unit for the visually handicapped of India. But to take it on himself was more than he felt he could do.

'It needs someone younger.' The conversation came to an end at this point, as one of them said, 'Let's pray about it.' So they prayed. Their prayers were urgent and spontaneous. The need of those blind people in India longing for the Word of God. The amazing possibility of swift production, with this computer programme that Don had devised. Oh, that the Lord would raise up someone of his own choice to take advantage of this opportunity! Oh, that he would direct to the right place for the unit to be set up! Should it be Bexhill?

And then, as they were praying, Rona had a vision. Sitting quietly in the Rogers' lounge, she found herself suddenly transported back to Moreton-hampstead along a narrow pavement leading to the centre of the little town, and to a deep porch in what seemed to be a cream coloured building. She had passed it innumerable times, but had never seen it clearly. Now, in her vision, she saw it distinctly, a deep porch, and in the wall beside it four tall, arched windows.

She knew what it was. She had gone through the porch several times, making her way along the narrow passage that led to a cottage at the back, where Bud and Rosemary Young lived. They owned the whole building, but it was disused, and had been so for a very long time. The tall, arched windows were never lighted now, the gallery was empty.

The vision of the porch and the arched windows was so clear and so unexpected that Rona could not ignore it. They had been praying, asking God to direct to his place for a braille unit, as well as someone to run it. Was this vision his answer? Rather hesitantly she said, 'There's a disused Methodist Chapel in Moretonhampstead.'

For Tony, this was the second shock on that memorable occasion. It seemed to bring the rather airy-fairy discussion right down to earth. The disused Methodist Chapel right there in Moreton-hampstead was uncomfortably close – in Moreton-hampstead! Nothing more was said about it, but in their next letter to their prayer partners, which was almost entirely about the work in India, a short paragraph at the end read,

'Finally, please keep on praying for the computerised production of Scripture for India. Don Rogers has completed his programme to get braille from the Devanagari (Hindi, Marathi and Nepali) script, and once we have obtained disks of the Hindi Bible, production can start. But where?' Then followed the question that began to localise prayer.

'Producing the Bible in the main languages of India is going to be a huge and ongoing project, so should a production unit for third world countries be established here?'

Shortly after that letter had been typed and mailed, as usual, by Sue Relf, Tony and Rona were surprised to receive a telephone call from London. The voice at the other end announced who was speaking – it was one of their blind supporters, quite a poor woman – and then went on to say, very definitely, that she believed they should go ahead. Then came another phone call, also from a blind friend, living in North Devon. She, too, urged them to set up the braille unit, right there in Moretonhampstead. Their prayer partners were evidently taking the matter very seriously, and Tony realized something must be done. He and Rona agreed to approach their friends, Bud and Rosemary Young about it. If they set up a braille unit, could the disused Methodist Chapel be rented to accommodate it?

The response was immediate and enthusiastic. Of course! Not only would he rent it to them, Bud said, but he'd have the whole place renovated, free of charge. He and Rosemary had always wanted the property, which had been set apart originally for the worship of God, to be used in his service.

There remained only one matter to be settled now, and Tony admitted later that he had expected it to bring the whole idea to an end. The Dartmoor National Park's authority was unquestionable in such cases as this. If this important body refused permission for the Chapel building to be used as a braille production unit, that would be final. It was most unlikely that permission would be given, especially as it meant installing machinery in a residential area. So the Dartmoor National Park's permission was sought, with very little expectation on Tony's part that it would be granted.

It was with mixed feelings that he eventually received official approval for the Methodist Chapel to be used for the production of Christian literature in braille. Just about the same time he had received a letter from the United Bible Societies, in answer to one that Don Rogers had sent to them, explaining that they could not produce computerised braille Bibles for India – but that *the need remained.*

'I realized that God was pushing me into it', Tony often said later. And since God's commands are always God's enablings, he knew he must go quietly but steadily forward.

One encouraging thing emerged when the Trust Deed was produced and studied, giving evidence of the Lord's fore-knowledge and planning. The clause which the solicitor had so surprisingly included, entitling the Trust to produce Christian literature in braille was now completely justified. Without it legal complications would undoubtedly have arisen, but, as it was, nothing further was needed for the new branch of the work to be included in FVH.

All the same it was a period of alternating hope and alarming apprehension – with more apprehension than hope most of the time. Their apprehension was shared by others, as they learned later. The minister of the church they attended was on holiday when their letter outlining what was needed to launch the project arrived, and as he read it through he started adding up in his mind what it was all likely to cost. The amount came to something in the region of £90,000, and he put the letter down on his desk impatiently, thinking, 'This is ridiculous! Wherever is such an amount of money coming from?' It was beyond human reason to expect it. He put the letter aside, and turned to read his Scripture Union notes for that day. To his amazement the words that headed it were, 'With God all things are possible.' He gave a little start, conscious that he was being rebuked. The words had come with startling clarity so promptly after what he had been thinking that he knew the message was from God himself. It was as though the Lord was saying to him, 'Do you believe this?' With the question there came to him a measure of faith, and he was able to reply with humble penitence, 'Yes, Lord, I do believe.'

Then the surprising thought came to him that Tony and Rona might be needing the same encouragement, so he picked up the phone and dialled their number. Rona's voice answered and she heard him say, 'I've just been reading Scripture Union notes for today, and the message is "With God all things are possible." I'd been thinking of you both, and felt the message was meant for you as well.' And he rang off, leaving Rona almost in tears. God knew what she and Tony had been feeling, and he cared. He did not send a word of rebuke, but rather a fatherly reassurance that he was with them, and they were on the right lines.

They needed that reassurance, although provisions were forthcoming in a variety of ways. A second-hand wiring machine was provided free of charge, and a second-hand paper cutter for one third of the usual price. A paper punch worth £5,000 was sold at half the price because it was the last of a discontinued line. Desks, tables, chairs for the office were given by friends who had no further use for them. Gifts of money came from unexpected sources (including £500 from the blind lady in North Devon), so the bank balance slowly increased – but it was far below what was needed to pay for the most expensive item of all – the Braillo itself. This was to come from Norway, and the price negotiated was £52,000 – half of which must be paid when the order was placed. And there was only about £3,000 in the bank.

The situation seemed hopeless, when out of the blue Tony received a letter from Arthur Pont, General Secretary of Interserve. He always received the Gibbs' quarterly letter, and having read their latest one he had a suggestion to make. Why not apply to Tear Fund for help? The fund sometimes supported literature projects, providing they were for the Third World. The Gibbs had never thought of it, but after prayer decided to get in touch with that well-known organization. A donation of £10,000 was received for the braille project for India. . . .

Then someone made another suggestion. Sir John Laing, the celebrated Christian philanthropist, had founded five different Trusts, one in the name of

Beatrice Laing. Could the Beatrice Laing Trust help towards providing Bibles in braille for India? Another £10,000 was donated. In answer to prayer, the needs were being met.

But there was another need, of an entirely different nature – the need for personnel. It was to be a constantly recurring need in the years that lay ahead, the need for the right people to do the right jobs, but in those early days the primary, outstanding need was for someone to work the Braillo when it was installed. It was a specialized job, and Rona knew that without the right person to do it the whole project would be held up. She had a weekly appointment for prayer with a friend living locally, Janette Brown, and decided to share the need with her, so that together they could claim the promise, 'If two of you shall agree on earth as touching anything that they shall ask in my name, it shall be done for them of my Father which is in Heaven.'

So they prayed, asking for the one of God's choice to be forthcoming to be responsible for working and servicing the Braillo. And here again it was revealed that months before this time, a quiet preparation had been made of the right person. The right person proved to be Janette's own husband.

Steve Brown was fully employed as Senior Engineering Instructor at the Royal National Institute for the Blind Training Centre at Manor House, Torquay. He had been there for years, with no thought of working elsewhere until in church one Sunday the preacher concluded his sermon by issuing a rather unusual challenge to his congregation. If the Lord called any of them to a complete change in their lives, to serve him in a new way, were they ready to do so? If they were, the preacher invited them to go and talk to him. Steve and Janette Brown were among those who went forward.

Nothing much happened after that. Certain changes in the Institute were likely to be made, and Steve knew that there was the probability of his obtaining a better paid job in it, for which he was quite prepared. Then his wife came home one day to tell him about the need which Rona Gibb had shared with her – the need for someone to work the Braillo the Gibbs were planning to have installed in the old Methodist Chapel in Cross Street, to produce Bibles in Indian languages for blind people in India.

His reaction to the news was prompt and perhaps not surprising. 'I'd like to be involved in something like that', he said. God was taking them at their word and leading them into a new work. He lost little time in going to see Tony to find out more about it. The outcome of their discussions was that Steve accepted early redundancy instead of applying for the higher paid job in the Institute, and became the first staff member, and manager, of the newly formed organization called Compass Braille. This name was chosen by a prayer partner, condensed from <u>COM</u>puterised <u>P</u>roduction of <u>AS</u>ian <u>S</u>cripts, its full title.

But before the Braillo was even installed, or the work started in Moretonhampstead, Steve and Janette Brown went, for the first time in their lives, to India.

The occasion of this visit, made with Tony and Rona, was to attend the 10th anniversary meetings of the founding of the India Fellowship for the Visually Handicapped in that country. They were introduced very early to the sort of delays that Tony and Rona were quite accustomed to. Their plane reached Madras at 2.30 a.m. on 19th October instead of 3.15 p.m. the previous day. There were further delays in getting the Word Processor they were bringing with them through Customs, 'but after many hours of negotiations with various Customs men at opposite ends of Madras City, we only had to pay £430 duty instead of the original £1,000 asked for.'

They had been met by members of the IFVH staff in Madras, and were taken to stay in a Christian guest house attached to a Theological College, and the following evening attended the first of the 10th Anniversary meetings that had been arranged. It was pouring with rain – the monsoon was at its height, and Tony and Rona warned the Browns that as people didn't usually come out after dark in the monsoon, there might not be many people at the meeting. In the event, to their surprise, the Church Hall was full to overflowing, with some 300 people present. Blind and sighted people were there, and the meeting took the form of a thanksgiving service for work now going on among the sightless people of India.

Looking back to the occasion in 1979 when Chandapilla had introduced an unknown English couple, Tony Gibb and his visually handicapped wife, to the Board of the Fellowship of Evangelical Churches in India, it was amazing to see how the work had expanded. The anniversary booklet that had been produced included a map of the whole country, marking the areas in which something had been done through the churches to reach the blind. Not one State had remained unvisited within the past year. In six cities Fellowship Centres were already established, in ten States Fellowships Camps had been held, in seven Seminar Workshops, and in three States there were Training Centres. Prabhu had travelled widely, and news of what was going on among blind people in India was reaching overseas. Prabhu had received an invitation from Joni Eareckson to attend a conference in the USA, he told the Gibbs, and both he and Nancy were becoming increasingly concerned about the plight of blind people in other countries of Asia. They felt they should extend their activities beyond the bounds of their own land.

The IFVH staff in Madras had planned the meeting well. They were not only looking back on what had been accomplished, but were looking forward as well. And they knew wherein their strength and inspiration lay. They had prepared an impressive banner which was to be used not only in this preliminary meeting, but in others that were to be held in Pune, Bombay, Ahmadabad, Nagpur. On it were the words,

TO GOD BE THE GLORY
GREAT THINGS HE HATH DONE.

14

Bringing God's Word to the Blind in Asia

When Tony and Rona returned from the 10th anniversary celebrations in India they realized that it was as if a chapter in their lives had closed and another one had opened. India was no longer their home and the centre of their lives. Their presence was no longer needed there now. The Camps, the opening of Fellowship Centres, the holding of seminars and workshops were all continuing without them. They might have agreed, if they had thought of it, that they were back where they had started – not at square one, but at six dots. They had gone to India in the first place to set up a braille unit, and now they were setting up a braille unit again, back in their own country – braille – six dots.

Setting up a braille unit was one thing, and for Tony it was simple enough. Launching an entirely new project, Compass Braille, with all that was involved, was another, and they both knew how it should get started.

'We must have a service of dedication,' they said. And they set about arranging it. It involved a good deal of correspondence and interviews, but when the day came, Wednesday, 30th May, 1990, the attendance at St. Andrew's Parish Church, Moretonhampstead was greater than anything they had anticipated. People came from far and near, and were placed in the aisles, and after the Rector had given the opening welcome and announced the first hymn the words rang out loud enough to drown the notes of the organ,

> O for a thousand tongues to sing
> My great Redeemer's praise . . .

Prayer, a Bible reading and another hymn were followed by greetings from the United Bible Societies in Stuttgart, Germany, conveyed in person by Miss Dorothea Kindt, the Braille Coordinator. Mr. Prabhu Rayan brought greetings from the India Fellowship for the Visually Handicapped, Madras, also in person. The Prayer of Commissioning was offered by the Minister of the East Dartmoor Baptist Church, and the address was given by the Rt. Rev. A. J. Dain, Assistant Bishop of Sydney, Australia.

There was something especially poignant to the Gibbs about the Bible reading – not only because it was the story of blind Bartimaeus, but because it was read by the blind friend from north Devon who had 'phoned them months before' urging them to com-

mence the work in Moretonhampstead. As she stood
there, clearly enunciating the words as her fingers ran
over the braille gospel before her, she symbolized the
purpose of all they were doing.

The service ended with the singing of the hymn
that started with the words on the banner used on
the 10th anniversary meetings in India,

> To God be the glory,
> great things He hath done . . .

The other blind friend who had 'phoned them was
also among the people present that day. A social
worker had accompanied her from London for this
special occasion, and she had brought with her a gift.
It was £300 that she had made through knitting dish
cloths and selling them at coffee mornings, bazaars,
sales of work, anywhere, to anyone who would buy
them at 50p each to help bring God's Word to blind
people in India.

*And Jesus sat over against the treasury and saw how
people cast their money in . . . and a certain poor
widow . . . cast in more than they all.*

* * *

Although the Commissioning service marked the
official opening of Compass Braille, work had
already been started a couple of weeks before with
Scriptures and books being produced in English and
Hindi. Among the books was one entitled *Dr.*

Sheela's Search for Peace, the story of a Hindu girl who found herself wondering why people in the temple were praying to a stone idol. The book was in English, and sent to a blind person in India. But the book did not stay in India. Blind pen friends were glad to exchange reading material, so Sheela Gupta's story, after being read in India, was sent to a pen friend in Hong Kong. When news came through that the Hong Kong pen friend had been converted as a result of reading the book, there was great rejoicing in Moretonhampstead. Such early and unexpected fruit seemed like a seal of divine blessing on the newly started work.

By the end of the year it was quite a common thing to see loads of boxes being conveyed to the Post Office from the Compass Braille building in Cross Street. All the manual work was being done by volunteers, the paper cutting, binding, wiring, boxing, loading onto the van – local friends who came along to give their services willingly.

But a lot more was going on behind the scenes, for the aim was to produce Bibles in braille in all the major Indian and other Asian languages, and this is what proved difficult. Where were the people who knew those languages sufficiently well to take on the laborious job of typing out, word for word, one of the books of the Bible? And then, where were four others with the same knowledge who could do the proof reading? The process of getting even one book produced in braille in a new language was a long and tedious business, and it had to start with finding the necessary linguists. Tony spent hours in the office, writing round to people he knew who had been in India, learnt one of the languages, were now back in this country and who would be willing to take on the jobs involved. He did not confine himself to missionaries, either. He thought of some of the Indians who had come to the U.K. on one pretext or another, and had landed up in jail. He knew that prisoners were getting a lot of computer training in prisons so if their skills could be utilized it could serve a double purpose. Not only would the Scriptures be produced in an Indian language, but the Indian prisoner would be introduced to the Word of God. In the course of his investigations Tony did hear of a Gujurati speaking prisoner in one of the jails, and a start was made with him – but then he was deported, and that was the end of that. A former missionary who knew Gujurati was contacted, too – but he went to the USA, and another hope was dashed. For a long time, the only portion of the Word of God in the Gujurati language was one of the gospels, which had already been produced in USA.

Productions in Hindi were more easily obtained, and very early a steady flow of new books in this language started. Margaret Robinson, an Interserve missionary who had been working in Pakistan, was back in the U.K. to care for her bed-ridden mother, and Hindi was the language she was prepared to type in. Very gladly she agreed to do the work involved, and as Don Rogers had already produced a computer programme for the language she set to without delay. It was perhaps the most encouraging feature of the work at that time, for otherwise there was so much going on in the office for which there seemed little to show. Letters and telephone calls kept Tony so busy that even with voluntary secretarial help it was evident a permanent member of staff was needed, so Maureen Watkins became a salaried member of Compass Braille. But still no new Indian languages were being introduced, and one reason for it was becoming evident. Compass Braille must have its own computer programmer. Had Don Rogers lived nearer, and been less involved with other projects, the need would not have arisen. Of his ability, and his willingness to help there was no question, but living in Bexhill, hundreds of miles away, and being in so much demand because of his skills, it was unreasonable to expect him to be involved only in Compass Braille and that was what was needed. In 1990 the autumn letter that Rona wrote to the Compass Braille prayer partners contained a specific request. Someone was needed who was qualified to write a computer programme to change Asian scripts into braille. The partners were asked to pray about this. A few days later the telephone rang, and the voice at the other end announced it was Simon Bartlett speaking. They knew him well. They had met him first in India, where he was on a missionary education programme with Interserve, prior to going to University. He explained that having received the prayer letter and seen the need for a computer programmer, he wondered, 'Would you consider a Sri Lankan girl working in Dubai, who wants to use her computer skills in some Christian work? She has recently been qualified, and I think she'd be willing to come, and is working now with a firm in Dubai.' Simon, it seemed, felt he could recommend her.

A Sri Lankan girl. She would need a work permit, and they were warned that it could take months to obtain. There were other considerations, too. How would a young woman from Asia fit into life in a remote little town in Southwest England? But correspondence was reassuring, prayer about it all brought peace of heart and mind, and so the work permit was applied for – and to everyone's surprise it came through in ten days. She had just enough time to give a month's notice to the firm in Dubai for which she was working, and in April 1991 the Gibbs motored to Gatwick airport to meet their new member of staff – Priscilla Balasingh. During the summer she went to stay with Professor and Mrs. Don Rogers to receive her training for the specialized job, and returned in the autumn ready to start in earnest.

Meanwhile, another financial crisis was looming up. The owner of the Chapel, Bud Young, had been advised by his bank manager to sell the property, and if it passed into other hands, who could tell whether Compass Braille would still be accepted as tenants? Tony and Rona were really dismayed. Money was coming in sufficiently to meet all the running expenses, but to buy a property worth about £75,000 made a demand on their faith that they felt unable to respond to. There was only one thing to do – it was what they had become accustomed to doing. They shared their dilemma with their prayer partners. Should they, or should they not, go ahead and say they would buy the property?

The response was overwhelmingly in favour of going ahead and buying. A few were dubious, but the vast majority of those who responded to their question were in favour of it. One prayer partner 'phoned and offered £10,000 as a gift. By November they had agreed with the Trustees to buy the property at the cost of £75,000. Gifts were beginning to come in – some small, some as interest free loans. There was one that specially touched Rona. She had been worrying, thinking about the Compass Braille staff. What if paying for the property meant that their salaries would be affected, and there would not be sufficient to pay them? She had quite a bad night, thinking about it, and the next morning a letter arrived, with a cheque for £1,000. It was from a blind prayer partner in Walsall, who explained that he and his wife were more housebound than they had been, and didn't really need the money – so he was sending it towards the general funds. 'They didn't really need the money . . .' It brought tears to her eyes, tears of love and tenderness.

Larger gifts came, too, though not more precious. One day she and Tony were very busy at Sunnymead when a telephone call from Compass Braille informed them that people from Worthing wanted to see them. Rather reluctantly, they went. To their surprise, two prayer partners were there, and after brief greetings one of them said, 'I've come because the Lord has told me to lend you an interest free loan. How much do you want?'

How much did they want? Tony, not knowing how to reply, said facetiously, 'Half a million pounds!' A general laugh was followed by a more realistic conversation, in which the offer was made of £20,000 or £25,000. Tony said that £20,000 would be sufficient, and the money was paid over. (It was later made a gift.) In August 1992 the property was legally transferred to Compass Braille.

*   *   *

During that time another member of staff had been added. Geraldine Cox had heard about Compass Braille from the minister of Worthing Tabernacle, and when she went to see the Gibbs about their need for an administrator, she arrived in time for coffee, and left about 11 p.m. The outcome of this visit was that three months later she joined the staff, and to Tony's relief started by putting the office in order, using the filing systems and business methods that he had planned and this eased things considerably. The work by this time was growing to such an extent that it was hard to keep up with it.

Typists in different Indian languages were being found, and proof-readers, so that gradually the aim of producing Bibles in Indian and other Asian languages was being fulfilled. In 1991 2676 Bible volumes in *Hindi*, *Marathi* and English were sent out. This was increased to 6,450 volumes in 1992 with *Telugu* being added, and then in 1993 the number was almost doubled to 12,062 with the addition of *Gujarathi, Tamil* and *Nepali*. In 1994 *Malayalam* was added, with a further increase in production. Added to these thousands of booklets in these languages were despatched each year.

The local volunteers who did all this work were often in evidence, and met each other frequently, but the workers behind the scenes, those responsible for the production of the disks upon which everything depended, were scattered in different places throughout the U.K. There was the man from Dehra Dun working among Asians in Bolton, who both typed and proof-read Gujarathi; the ex-Dohnavur missionary, and the ex-Tear Fund worker who proof-read Tamil, the retired Interserve missionary who proofread Marathi, the elderly nun who proof-read Bengali, the eye-specialist contacted through the Officers' Christian Union who typed Hindi, the ex-Baptist missionary who typed Marathi, the couple whom Tony and Rona met in the dining room of the Foreign Missions Club in Highbury, London, who offered to proof-read and type Marathi and Tamil . . . And so on.

Rona, always alert to opportunities for hospitality, was in her element when once a year there was a Compass Braille volunteers' weekend in Moretonhampstead. As many as possible of these workers came and were crammed into Sunnymead, while friends in and around the little town opened their homes to others. Meals were served from behind the hatch in the primary schoolhall, and with sixty or more people sitting down at the tables there was a ceaseless babble of talk as friends who had been in

India met unexpectedly. The Compass Braille family weekend brought an added bonus to the satisfaction they all had in doing something, making a positive contribution to bringing the Word of God to blind people in Asia.

15

The Work Continues

Rona was sitting in the lounge at Sunnymead with Rajah flopped at her feet, his head between his two paws, waiting to be stroked. She was relaxing after a busy morning in the kitchen, making mince pies in preparation for Christmas, and had taken time off to review the past year's work at Compass Braille for the benefit of her visitor. She needed no notes – all the information was stored in her head. She sounded so encouraged. The output from Compass Braille had been greater than ever before; in fact, production had doubled in recent months.

A letter had recently been received from a blind Nepali speaking Indian Christian. Rona remembered what the letter had said. 'Thank you very much for the New Testament in Nepali braille. These two large precious boxes arrived here in good time. The last time I possessed a Nepali New Testament was forty-six years ago.' (Immediately after that he had lost his sight.) '. . .What a thrill it is to have the Lord speaking in your own mother tongue through the dots. Thank you, Lord, for the friends in Compass Braille.' This letter had obviously been such an encouragement to both Rona and Tony.

Rona explained that Tony had never been satisfied to work for blind people only in India – his vision was for the whole of Asia. To his delight consignments had been sent to Nepal and Bangladesh as well as to India. Work was also being done on new languages – Kannada, Oriya, Bengali and, for Sri Lanka, Sinhalese – and these were expected to be produced in the near future.

Work-wise things had gone fairly well, though not entirely without difficulties. One of the big problems had been connected with personnel, or rather the lack of them! Everybody likes a love-story, so when Priscilla, the invaluable computer programmer, explained that Simon Bartlett had asked her to marry him, and that she had accepted his proposal, what was there to say? Simon was the one who had first introduced her to Compass Braille. He was the catalyst who had brought her into the work – now the catalyst was taking her away from it. But after various discussions it had been agreed that after marriage she would remain on at Compass Braille, working three days a week, to fulfil the four years of her work permit. The Gibbs were thankful for that, although it still left a big gap very difficult to fill, for computer programmers were not easy to find – at least not computer programmers who were willing to take a cut in salary for the privilege of helping blind people in Asia to read the Bible.

However, there was one person already prepared, although they did not know him at the time. They were brought into touch with him by one of those happenings which some people refer to as 'coincidences' but others regard as divine guidance. They were attending an Officers' Christian Union conference held at High Leigh in Hertfordshire and another conference was on there at the same time. Delegates from the two conferences met only for evening drinks. On the first evening, Tony approached a delegate from the other conference to inform him that if anyone from their group wished to help themselves to free literature about Compass Braille they would be most welcome to take it. The astonished man stared at Tony's name-tab and gasped, 'Tony Gibb! Are you from Compass Braille? I've just written to you!' He went on to explain that he'd heard of the work and wanted to know more about it. His name was David Barnard. He was a computer programmer, and had worked in British Aerospace for some twenty years. Unexpectedly meeting the very man to whom he had written quickened his desire to see for himself what was going on, so he arranged to visit Moretonhampstead. The outcome of his visit was that he talked the matter over with his wife, they agreed that it was the Lord's guidance for David to join the Compass Braille staff, and although it would mean selling their house in Hertfordshire and moving to Devon, they were prepared for the uprooting that would be involved. It was not an easy decision to make, and a long delay in selling their home and finding a suitable one in an unfamiliar neighbourhood had tested their faith and their patience. But now, in December 1994, they were happily settled.

Another staff crisis had occurred during that year, when Geraldine Cox announced in May that she wanted to leave at the end of July to do research into the needs of visually handicapped people in the Middle East. Her practical contribution to the work of Compass Braille had been exceptional. As well as being a very able administrator in the office she was an excellent speaker. During her two years on the staff the number of volunteer typists and proof readers around the UK had increased from 30 to 160, largely due to her moving presentation of the ways in which the Compass Braille team in Moreton-hampstead were helping to satisfy the longing of blind people in India for the Word of God. Geraldine was missed – 'but', Rona mused, 'we were sure that if the Lord had called his servant to another field, we could look to him to fill her place. In an ongoing work one must be prepared for changes and emergencies.'

Her visitor agreed, but there were some aspects of the work about which she was still curious so, changing the subject slightly, she asked, 'Who distributes the books that are sent out from Compass Braille, and where do they go?'

'India Fellowship for the Visually Handicapped passes on a lot – books in Tamil, Marathi, Gujarathi, Hindi, Bengali and Nepali. We send them entirely free of charge to main distributors in India that we know. We don't send them ad lib, to anyone who asks and whom we don't know', Rona said. 'Another important distributor is Mission to the Blind, and we've known the founder, Sam Thanaseelan, since 1978. He has 30 members of staff distributing our Bible volumes and booklets. Then there's the Discipleship Centre in Delhi which distributes Hindi braille all over North India.

'The headmaster of the Mary Scott School for the Blind in Kalimpong, is a blind Nepali speaker. Over the years many ex-students have come to Christ, and he keeps in touch with them, during holidays, visiting them when possible in their homes in North East India and Nepal. He distributes Bible volumes and booklets to these people, most of them do not have any other Christian contacts, so our literature is what helps to keep them alive spiritually. Nepali literature in small quantities has also gone to the Secretary of the Nepal Bible Society in Kathmandu. Prabhu has some contacts in Nepal, and we hope to get a proper distribution network set up within the next year. We are ready to produce the New Testament in greater quantities, and some small booklets, when this is established.'

'Bibles going to India are channelled through the Bible Society of India. Sometimes we send these books to them and sometimes they request us to send them directly to the distributors already mentioned.'

Rona's visitor looked at her watch, and decided it was almost time she left, but she was still eager to hear about the trip to India from which Tony and Rona had just returned. Had they met Prabhu and Nancy? 'Yes, it was good to see them again', Rona replied.

No, they hadn't been able to meet Chandapilla, as he now lived too far away from any of the places they visited, and they were really sorry about that. He and his wife had meant so much to them in their early years in India. 'But we met a number of others, including Reggie Matthew, Director of Christian Foundation for the Blind, Kerala. We have had a close link with him since we met in 1978. His work is confined to Kerala, where he distributes Malayalam braille Scriptures to his contacts, which now number over 3,000. He has laboriously produced some volumes of the New Testament as well as Psalms. He is eager for us to produce the remainder of the Malayalam Bible, and also other literature. He gave us a lovely welcome', said Rona, adding reminiscently, 'And insisted on paying our hotel bill.'

It was good to have seen Sam Thanaseelan, whom they had known for fifteen years. He had been Director of India Youth for Christ, but had become so concerned to reach blind people that he resigned from YFC and in 1992 founded Mission to the Blind. He had recently visited Sri Lanka where there was a possibility of starting up a similar work among the visually handicapped people of that country.

Then there had been Shantijai Khristmukti, now Mission to the Blind Director in North India, who had first contacted the Gibbs in 1982, after he led a blind Hindu student to Christ. At that time he was pastor of a Methodist church, but his concern for blind people increased to such an extent that he eventually resigned from the pastorate of his church to give himself full time to working among them. 'He has struggled to produce a few booklets and Bible volumes for his hundreds of blind people eager to read the message of Christ. He is impatient for more Bible volumes, and wants more booklets too. . . .'

'We have so much to read ourselves', observed Rona's visitor, 'Biographies, magazines, devotional books. We take it for granted that we can go and get a Christian book to read any time we want one. But these people who have lost their sight – or never had it. . . . nothing to read.'

Rona knew from experience what that meant. She remembered how delighted she had been when she first went to Torch Trust for the Blind to discover the library of Christian literature there, that she had not known existed. And how she had longed, when she and Tony had arrived in India, for something over which her fingers could move for words that would feed her mind and her soul. 'Nothing to read. . .'

Jeanette Short had been conscious of that need years ago, and had started to produce a Hindi monthly magazine, called Deepak, which she later handed over to the Discipleship Centre in Delhi, and it now had a circulation of about 1,500. 'The workers in the braille department of the Centre have a strong postal link with their Deepak readers to whom they send tracts, booklets, portions of Scripture. Over the years a number have come to Christ through reading these Scripture portions. Many of them have no church link, as they are confined to their homes because their families are ashamed of having a blind member – what those sheets of embossed paper mean to them!'

Then there was Chandra Singh. She had assisted Jeanette in the running of the India Every Home Crusade Correspondence Courses, and was now completely responsible for them. Rona told her visitor, 'Over the years she has built up postal contact with 2,000 Hindi braille readers, to whom she distributes any Hindi Christian literature she can get... she pleaded with us to complete the Hindi Bible as soon as possible, and more booklets and testimonies which could be helpful for young Christians to grow in the faith.'

The morning was almost gone but Rona still had more to tell. She and Tony had returned from India with not only a sense of achievement but also a challenge for the future. There had been some exciting meetings. They had met an old friend who had a braille press. He shared with them his longing to produce more Bible volumes and Christian literature, but his equipment was not computerised. He asked Tony to look into the feasibility of adapting his manual press to enable him to use computer disks. He would then be able and delighted to accept Compass Braille disks, and production of Bibles could go ahead in India. Two other reliable groups also expressed an interest in producing braille Christian literature by computer and asked about the availability of suitable presses. This was thrilling. Tony had always longed to see the Christian Braille literature needed in India actually produced there. Now it seemed that the Lord was impressing this same desire on Indian Christians too.

Reluctantly Rona's visitor had to tear herself away. When she had gone, Rona put on her coat and went out. She walked up the narrow road to Cross Street and came to a porch beside which was a wall with four tall arched windows in it. It was a listed building, and outwardly was much as she had seen it in her vision six years before. There was now a brass plaque by the arch, announcing that this was Compass Braille. . . .

But as she stepped inside . . . . how different it all was! The large unused church of her vision was teeming with life. It now had three floors each abuzz with busy workers. There were offices and work-rooms with people writing, typing, programming, answering the telephone. . . There were two Braillo units in the basement, working away at top speed, churning out continuous sheets of embossed paper, stacking up in piles on the floor. There they waited to be transferred in the lift to the ground floor where voluntary helpers would cut, punch and wire them together into books. Labels, bearing the words BRAILLE – FREE POST, were being stuck on to boxes and two or three able bodied people were moving them out into the porch for loading on the vans that would convey them to the Post Office. There was not much talking going on, as everyone was busy attending to his or her particular job. The volunteers were housewives, retired people, senior citizens, young people with time to spare to give a hand at Compass Braille. Some of them lived in Moretonhampstead, others had come in from nearby villages or towns for an hour, two hours, half a day, once a week, twice a week, every day. . . The place was rather like a beehive, Rona thought, as she went in, greeted by one and another of the staff and volunteers who were there. They were like the worker bees, those who stayed in the hive out of sight, quietly making the cells without which there would be no 'comb'. . . and therefore no honey. . . .

So much had gone on prior to the achievement of getting the Word of God into the hands of blind people in India and beyond. There were the early pioneers, like Annie Sharp, who founded the first school for the blind, over a century ago. There were those who followed her, those who had a concern for the despised and rejected sightless ones, those who had learned the languages, those who like Don Rogers had used their exceptional skills to make possible the computerised production of braille Bibles in Indian languages, and then there was Tony, whose obedience to the Lord and whose practical skills had now made this vision a reality.

So here was Compass Braille – in a little town in Devon, but scattered all around the country Rona knew there were nearly two hundred volunteer typists and proof readers, working in their own homes, preparing the disks to be used here at the Press. Rona felt a tremendous surge of gratitude as she thought of those people, some personally known to her, some not, who worked away, day by day, on their own. Their perseverance was truly amazing and without them, and the volunteers here, the work would come to a standstill.

And what of the future. . . ?

Rona knew that neither she nor Tony wanted Compass Braille to be seen as a completed project. Under God's hand, who could tell how it might develop? There were so many possibilities. It could be that Compass Braille would become a pattern for many similar production units in Asia. . . .and then it might become a training centre for Asian nationals who wished to learn how to convert their own scripts into braille. . . .perhaps it would become a place where disks could be prepared for other countries wishing to produce their own braille Bibles. . . .Rona hoped that it would continue to be a place where braille Bibles and Christian literature are produced for any Asian countries in which such production is impossible. Above all, she hoped that God's will and purpose would always be earnestly sought and eagerly followed.

'Compass Braille as it is today is not the end of a story. . .', Rona thought, '. . . it is surely just the beginning!'